Where My Spirit Guides Us
Ancient Hula on the Big Island of Hawai'i

michael philip manheim
PHOTOGRAPHY

SEE-SAW

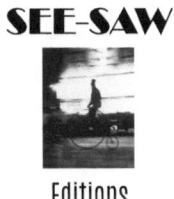

Editions

BY MICHAEL PHILIP MANHEIM

IN A LABYRINTH
LAST HOUSE STANDING, A Chapter
SEE-SAW, A Sampler
THE SMOKING FIFTIES
WHERE MY SPIRIT GUIDES US

These can be found on Amazon by entering Michael Philip Manheim into the search field

Where My Spirit Guides Us
Copyright © 2015 Michael Philip Manheim
Second Printing 2018

For further information or permissions, including the leasing of reproduction rights, go to
www.michaelphilipmanheim.com and click on "contact me"

Printed in the United States of America.
ISBN-13: 978-0-9844803-6-4

Preface

In this series of photographs, Michael Philip Manheim furthers his journey into the human heart and spirit. For years, he has invited brave souls to be photographed as they set into movement a release of their inner beings. His multi-exposure images reveal sophisticated portraits of a shadow self, interpreting the complexity of each Individual.

Now this approach has been applied to *Where My Spirit Guides Us.* The project celebrates the practice of ancient *hula*. Manheim has been photographing as Kumu Hula Ehulani Stephany guides her *hula hālau* (hula school) into channeling the spirits of their ancestors. The resulting photographs reveal stunning transformations. Manheim says, "I have never worked with a participant who equaled Kumu's transformative powers. For the viewer, it is hard at times to believe that it is truly the same woman from picture to picture."

Beyond sharing this powerful experience with a wider audience, the project aims to spotlight Kumu and her *hālau* mission. She avidly works to educate, preserve and promote the ancient art of *hula*, which she sees as central to the preservation of traditional Hawaiian civilization. Denigrated by colonizing invasions, western-imported disease and modern-day commercialization, these rituals and ritual spaces are in dire need of just such a champion.

Her work is not aimed at some greater glory. It is a labor of love. As Kumu writes of their efforts to restore ancient *hula* as well as Hawaiian *heiau* (temples): "We're not looking to receive any financial payment for this work, for it comes from deep within the heart and soul of me and all my *haumāna* (students) and other volunteers."

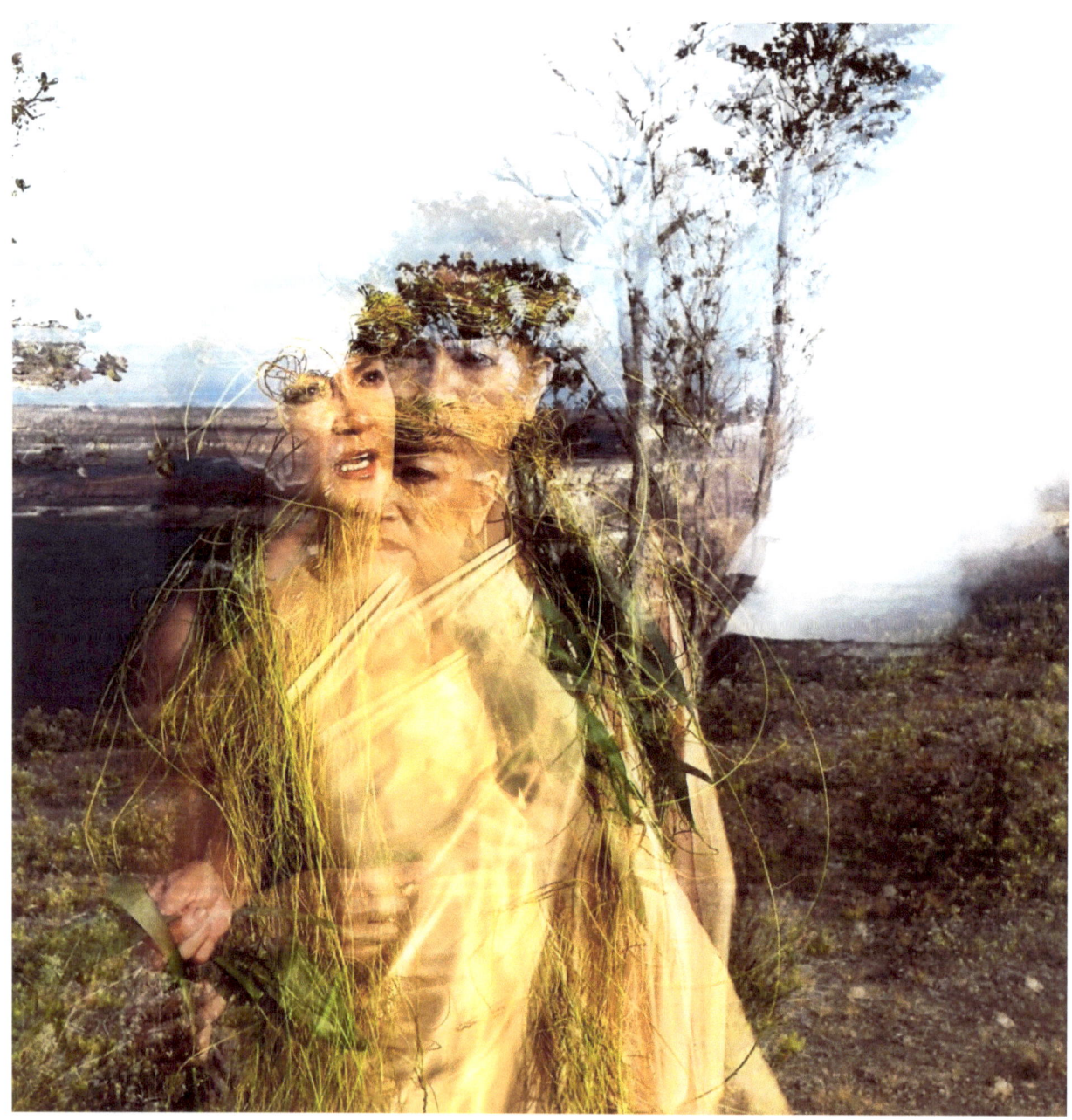

Ancient Hula

by Kumu Hula Ali'i Kahuna Nui Ehulani Stephany

Aloha, my name is Ehulani Stephany, and I'm a *kumu hula* (hula teacher) here on Hawai'i Island. I've been teaching traditional hula since 1990, and the name of my school is Halau Hula Ka Makani Hali 'Ala O Puna, which translates to The Returning Fragrant Wind Of Puna. We are from the district of Puna on the Big Island of Hawai'i.

Most visitors who come to the Hawaiian islands experience not our traditional *hula* (*hula kahiko*), but more often *hula 'auana* (modern hula), or a very *Waikiki* style of show. These schools tend to focus on competition and exhibition.

Our *hālau* hula is not like that. We focus on the protocols of our culture, and learning the traditional *hula* in the most *pono* (right) way as possible, along with learning how to make our own *hula* instruments, various types of *leis*, *hula* skirts, and arts and crafts of Hawai'i.

Our *hālau's* goal is the perpetuation of our Hawaiian culture. By learning the *hula kahiko* (ancient hula) and *oli kahiko* (ancient chants), we keep our culture alive, helping it to live on and become stronger, never to be forgotten.

Mahalo nui loa Michael, for all that you do.
Our Hawaiian ancestors really
trust and believe in you to continue to
reveal themselves in your wonderful photos.
A hui hou, Kumu

Where My Spirit Guides Us

Ancient *Hula* on the Big Island of Hawai'i

The *hula* is telling a story at all times, the hands, feet, head, facial expressions, and body movement are all part of the story. The chanter is chanting the story, while the *hula* dancer is expressing the story of the chant. And the history of the ancients becomes alive today.

The graceful hula hands are the softness deep within our Hawaiian people along with the story of the chant, the feet are keeping us in tune with our motions and grounding us as we move, the facial expressions are how we feel with the motions and meanings, the body moves to the nature of the flowing trade winds and the ocean that surrounds our islands.

— Kumu Hula Ali'i Kahuna Nui Ehulani Stephany

Transformation

Kumu Hula Ali'i Kahuna Nui Ehulani Stephany

The people viewing her images are astonished that all those different people are Kumu Hula Ali'i Kahuna Nui Ehulani Stephany. My multiple exposure exploration has featured transformations over the years, where people appear unlike their literal selves.

When they release from within and turn that into movement their monsters, their animals, and sometimes even their angels appear. But after perhaps a maximum of three sessions, all that each has to offer has been exhausted.

With Kumu, the transformations continue. It's understandable to her. She calls up the spirits. They guide her. And her ancestors come to light. Each session with Kumu and her *hālau* takes place at a sacred place on Big Island Hawai'i.

— Michael Philip Manheim

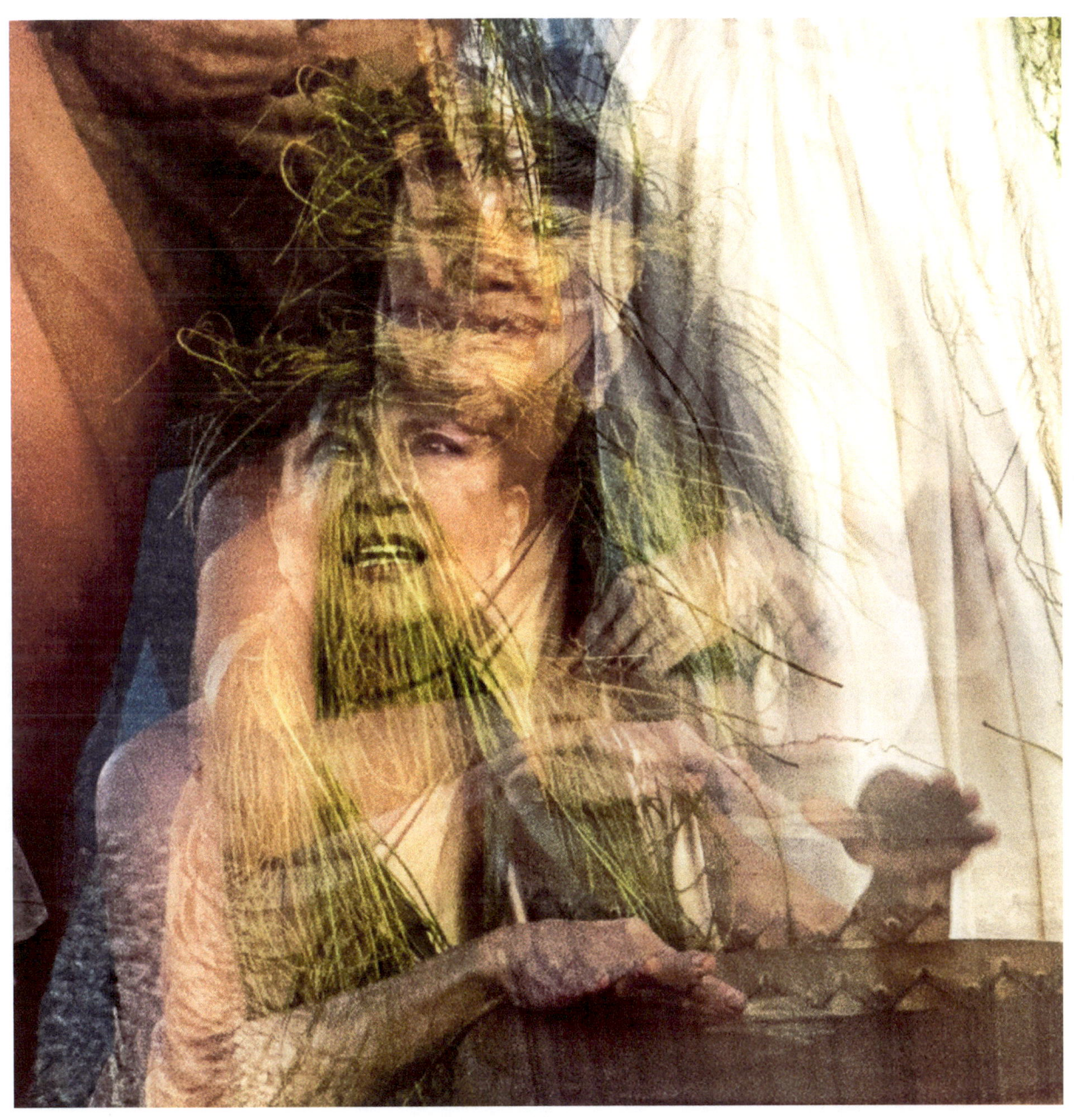

Kumu Hula Ali'i Kahuna Nui Ehulani Stephany

Voices of Our Ancestors
The Power of Sacred Spaces

These are photographs of Kumu and her students in the ancient practice of *hula* called *hula kahiko*. Her full title in Hawaiian is Kumu Hula Ali'i Kahuna Nui Ehulani Stephany, both teacher and high priestess. Unlike the *hula* most tourists see, ancient *hula* is a spiritual experience wherein the dancers commune with nature and ancestors. By teaching her practice Kumu aims to preserve the indigenous culture long threatened by colonization, disease, and westernization. These photographs attempt to capture the spiritual transformation brought about by the ephemeral and transcendent influences of ancestral voices.

— Michael Philip Manheim

8

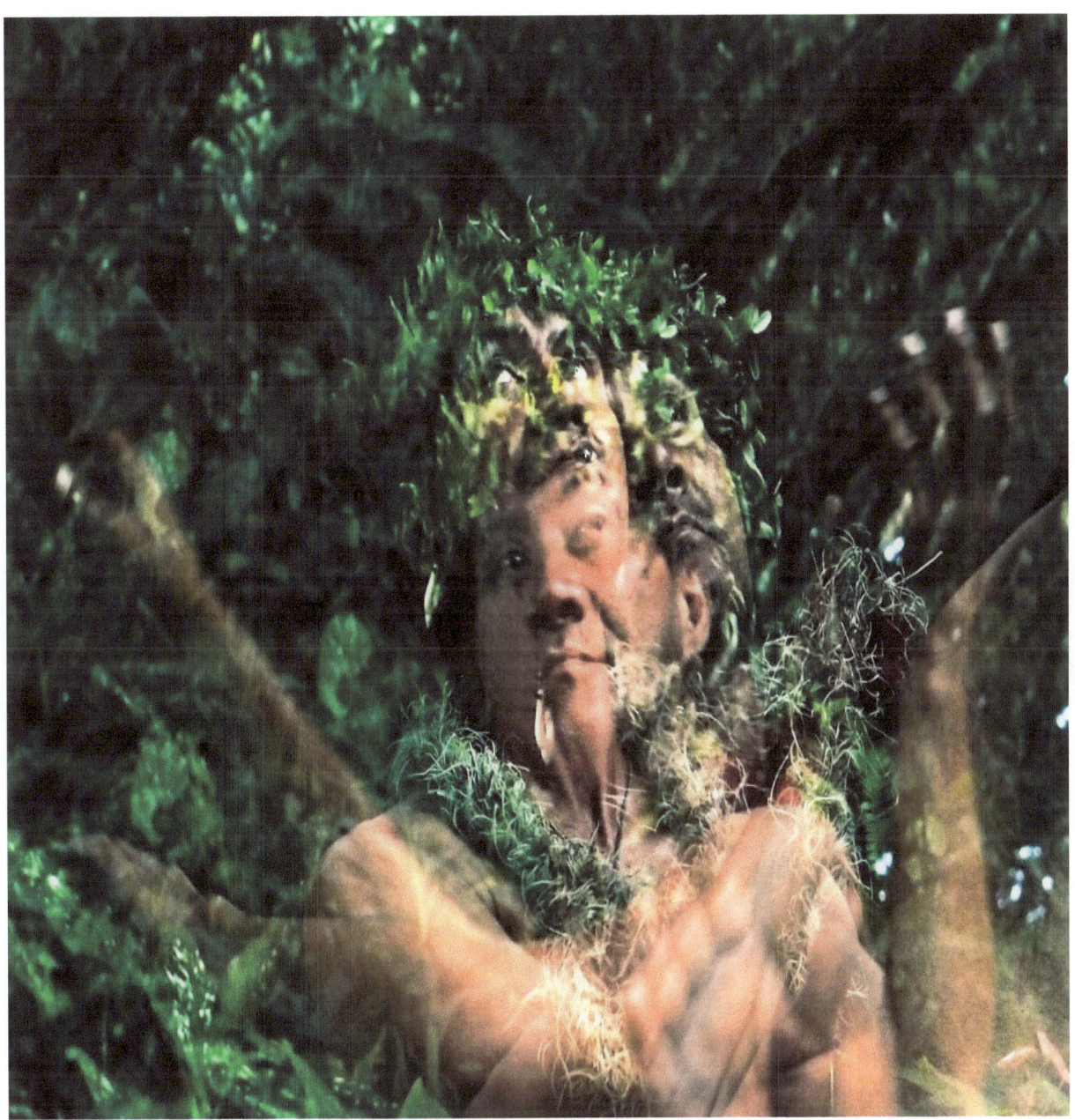

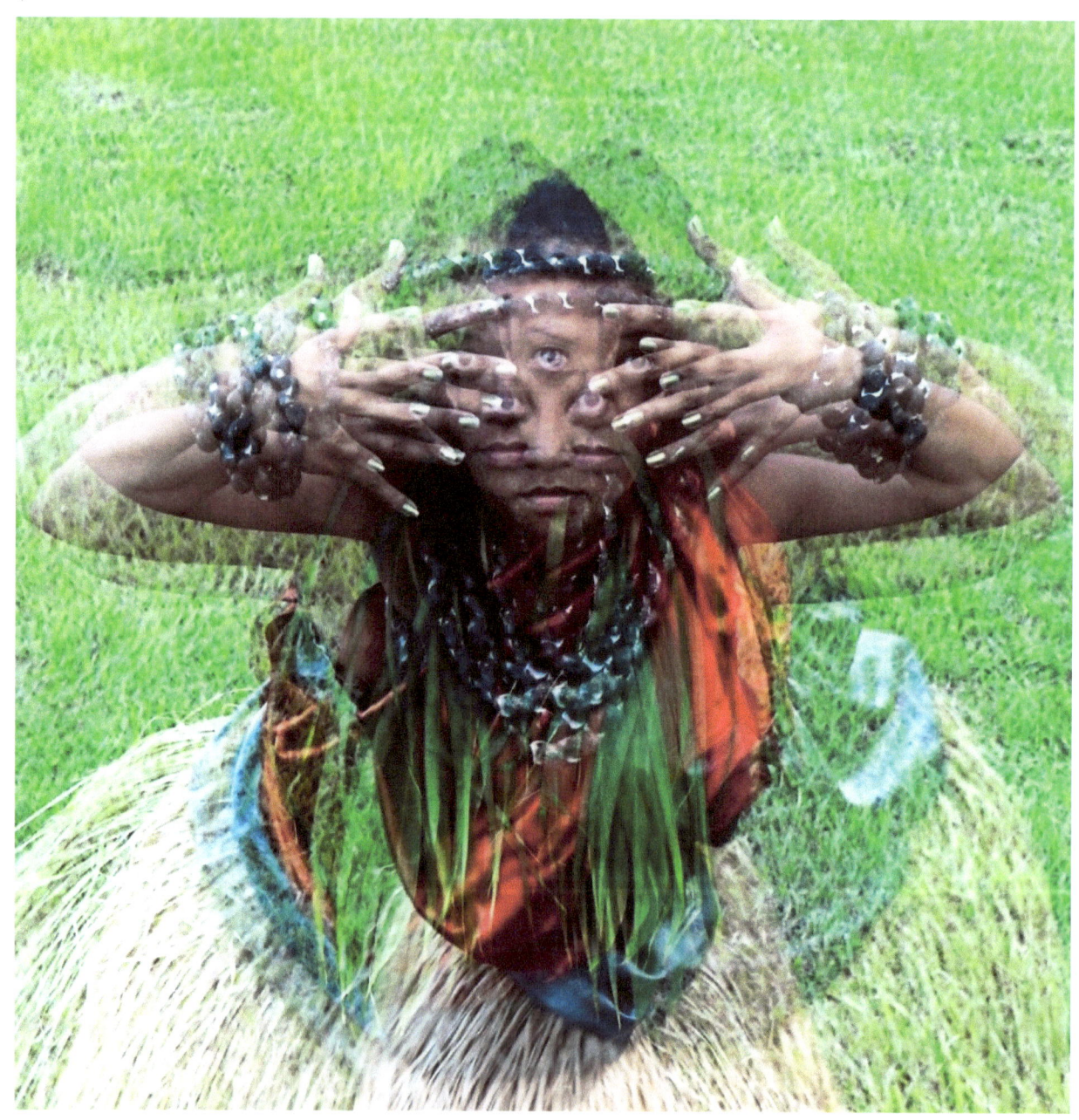

Sacred Areas

Locating the Spirit

Our photographic sessions took place in sacred spaces (exact locations cannot be revealed, in order to protect them), with Kumu guiding her students in connecting with their ancestors by connecting to the earth.

All went to their inner selves, releasing into movement that I reflexively captured in overlapping multiple exposures. These iterations went beyond the literal, into an interpretive and soulful response. As dancer Ulu expressed it, "Acknowledging my ancestors through the perpetuation of my culture, is in actuality . . . an expression of who I am."

Where Life Began

Chapter One

This is Pali ʻUli, the sacred waters of Kane, located in the Puna district of Hawaiʻi. Many songs, chants, and hula mention this sacred area, with great honor and respect, because it is believed to be where life began. As expected, Kumu connected with ancestors who revealed themselves.

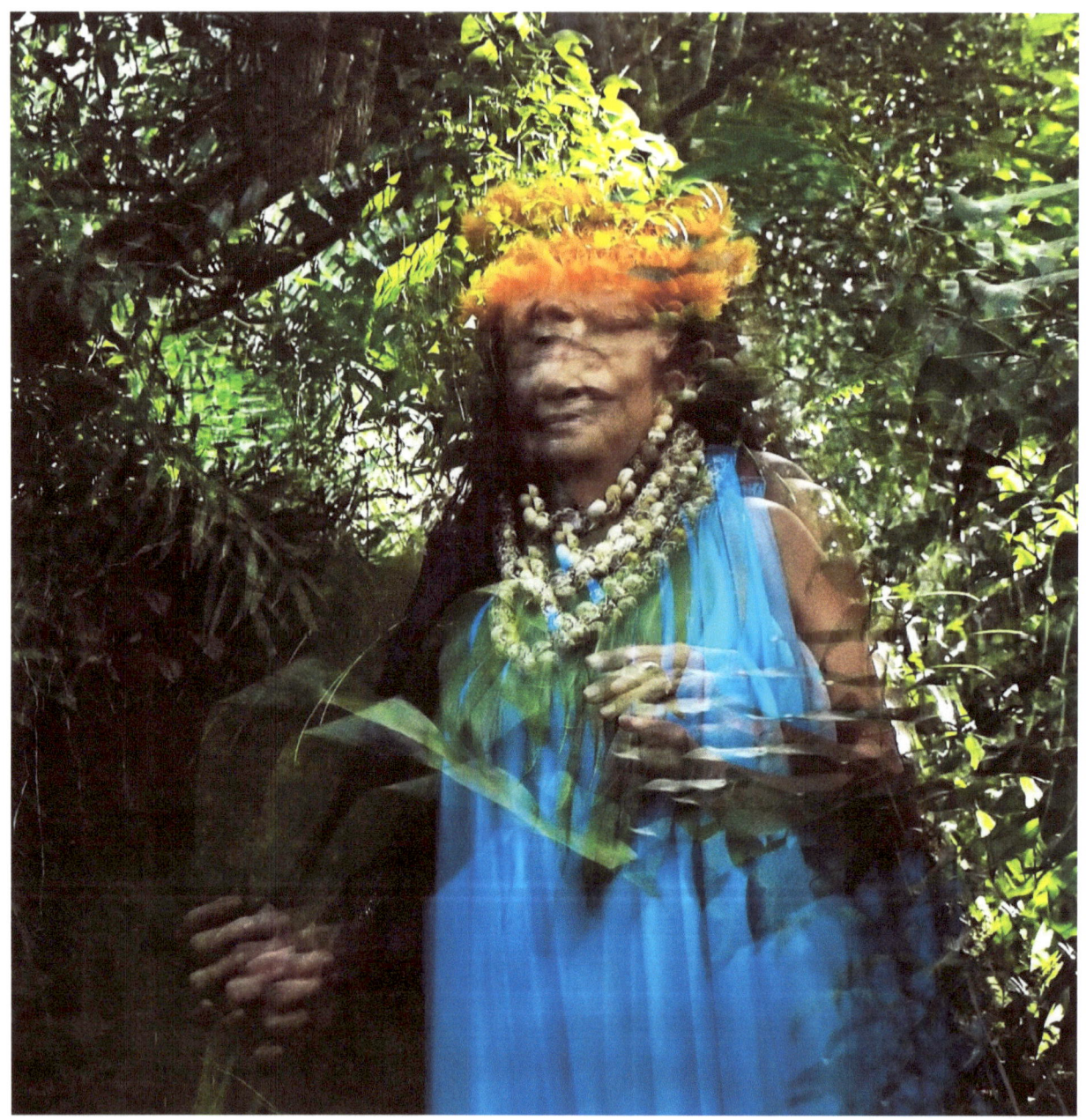

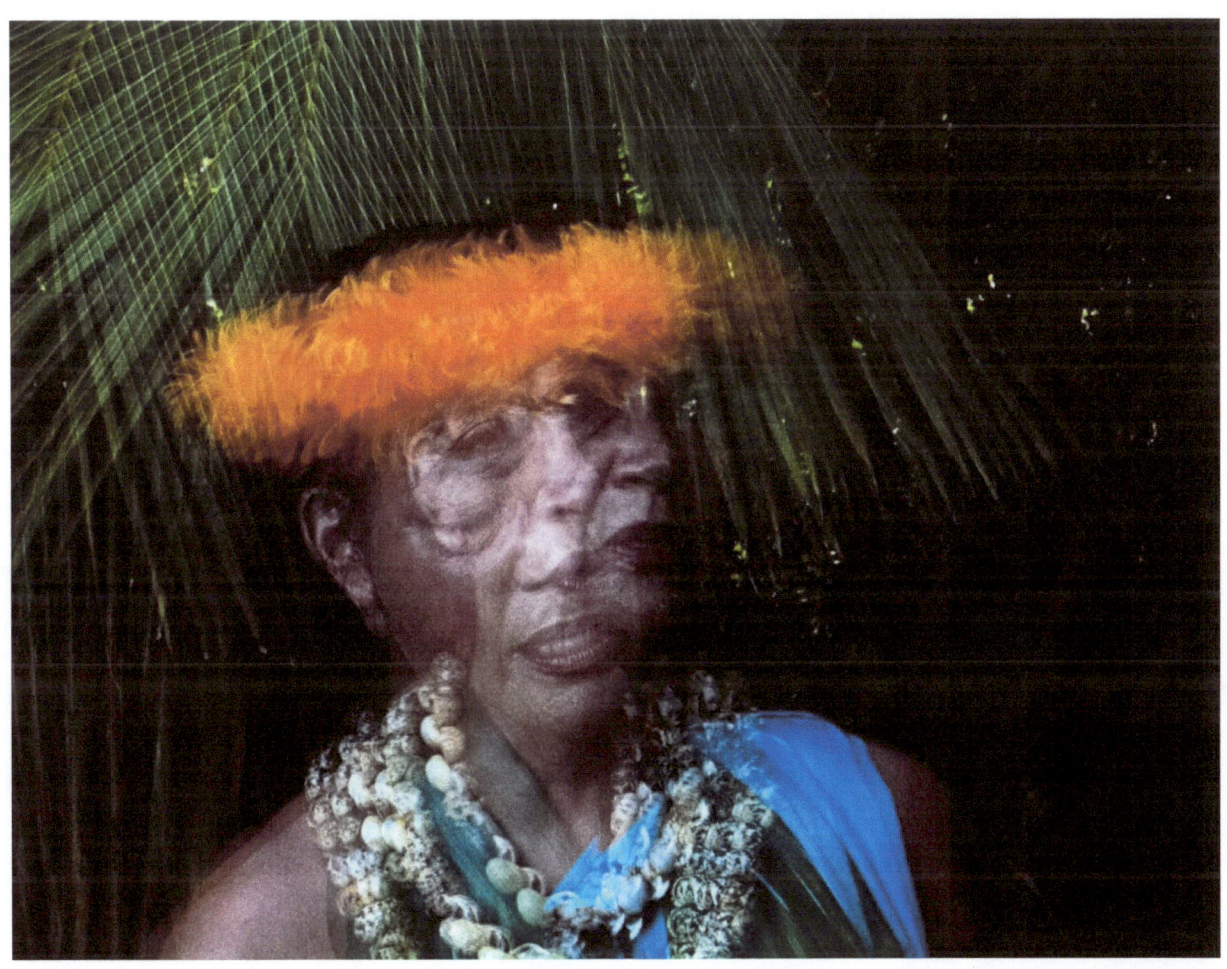

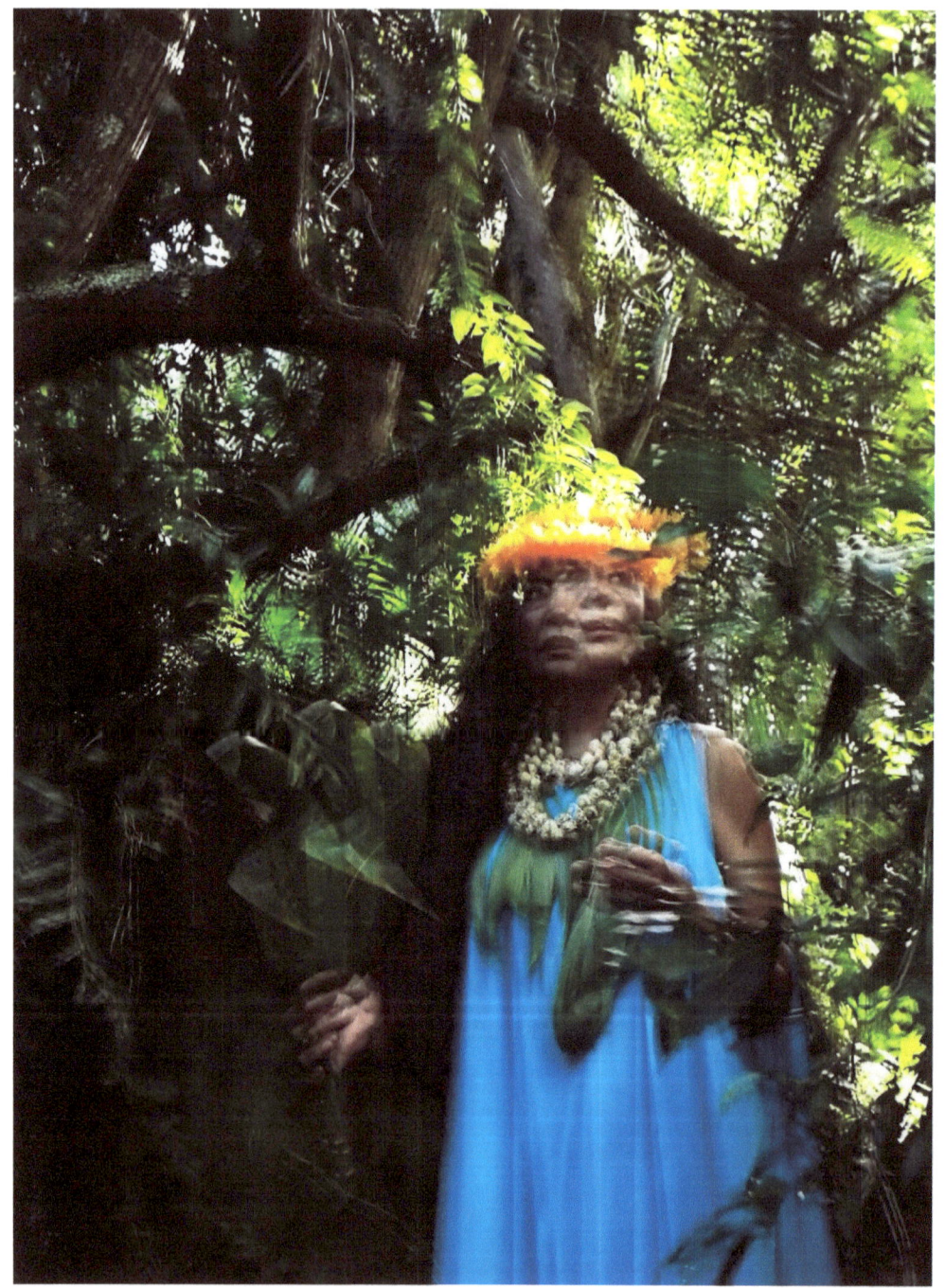

16

Ancient Village

Chapter Two

This is Waʻa Waʻa, an ancient village area, where many Hawaiian people of long ago lived and died. By common consent, they gave up their lives. Meeting with chiefs from all over the island, they decided to never leave their villages after becoming infected. In doing so, they protected the rest of the indigenous people from the many diseases brought by foreigners who came to the islands. They are now buried where we photographed, having lived out their lives there.

It is thought that measles alone killed 30,000 islanders in this region. All that is left is jungle, where villages once stood.

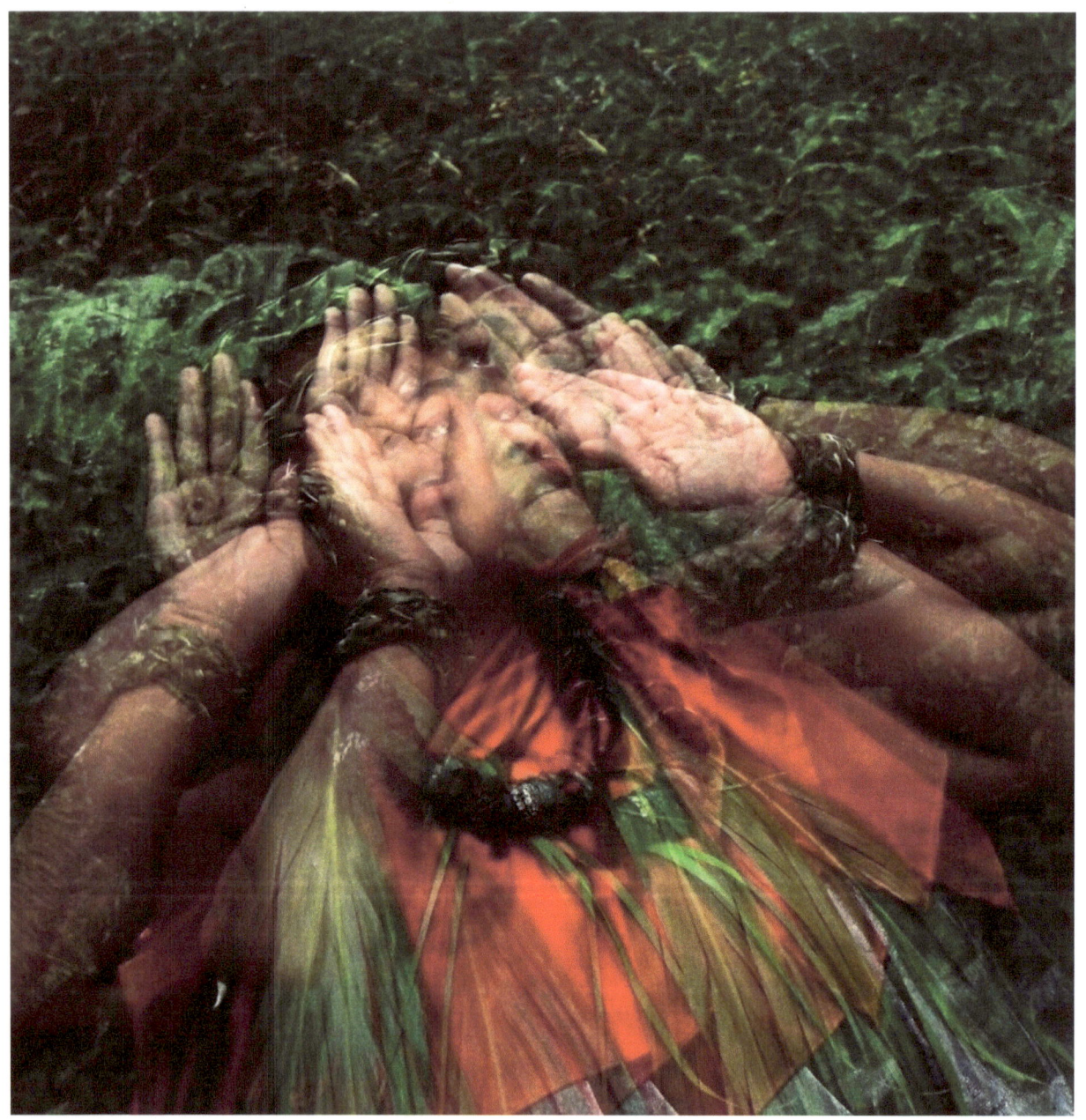

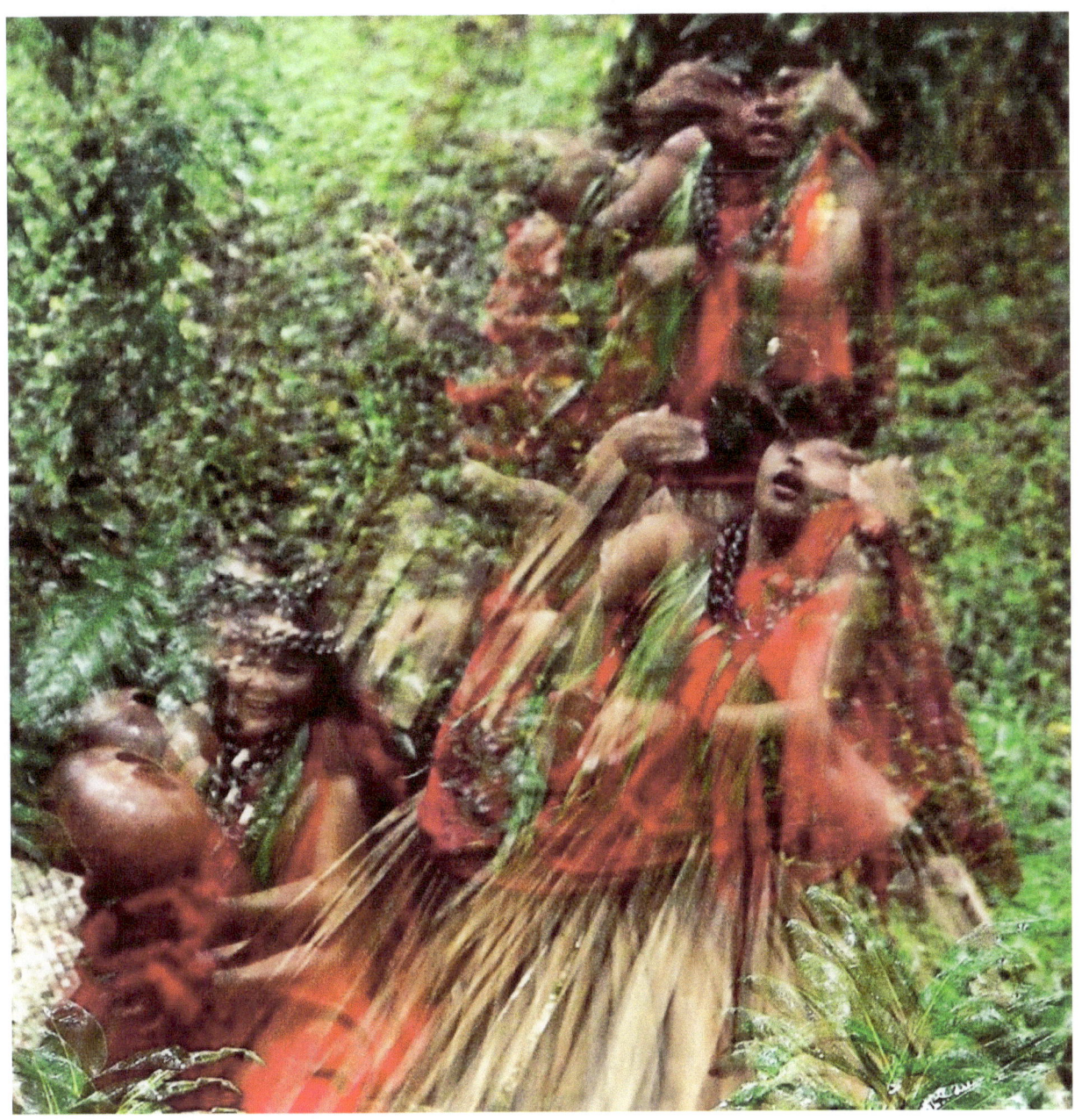

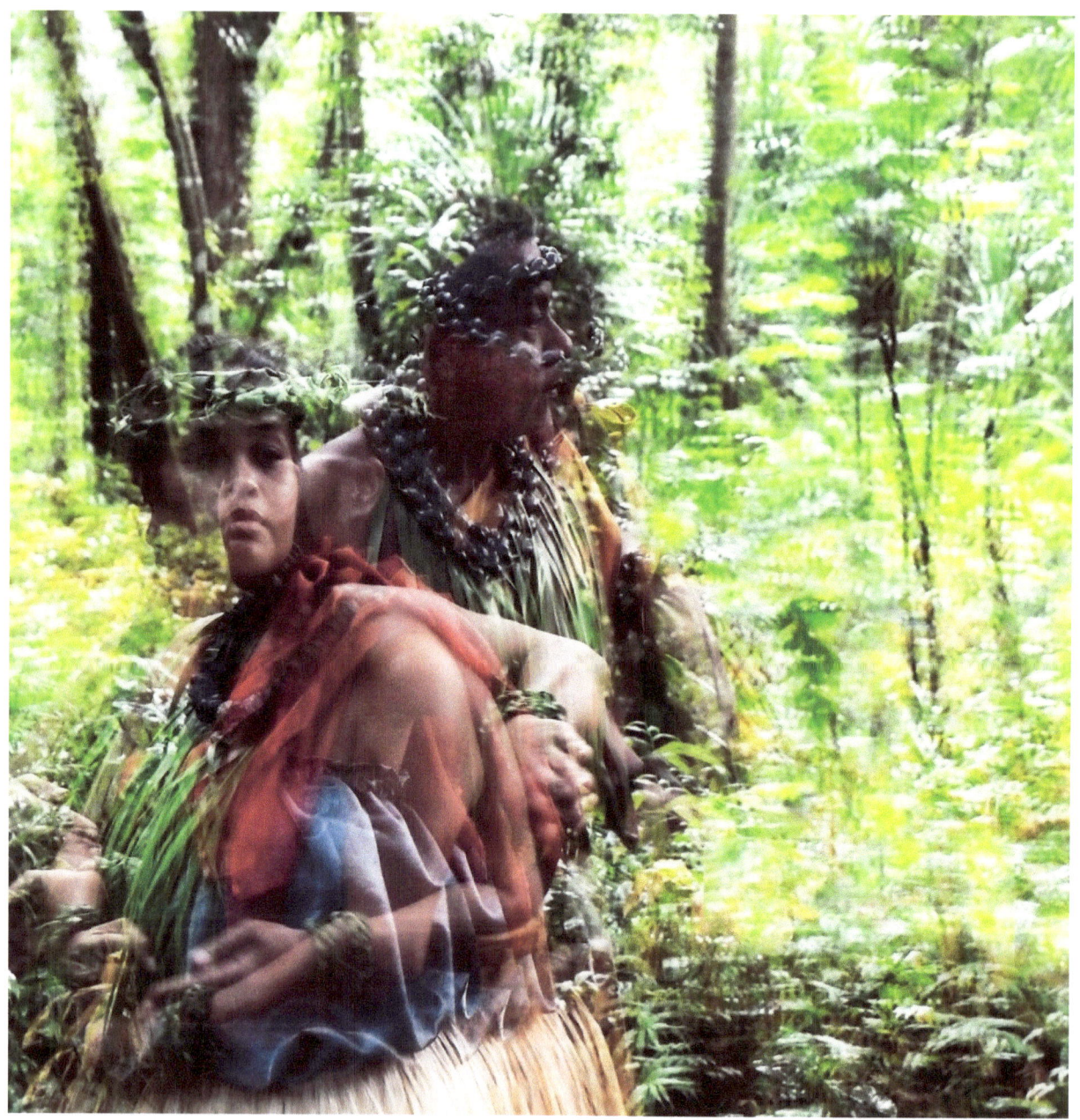

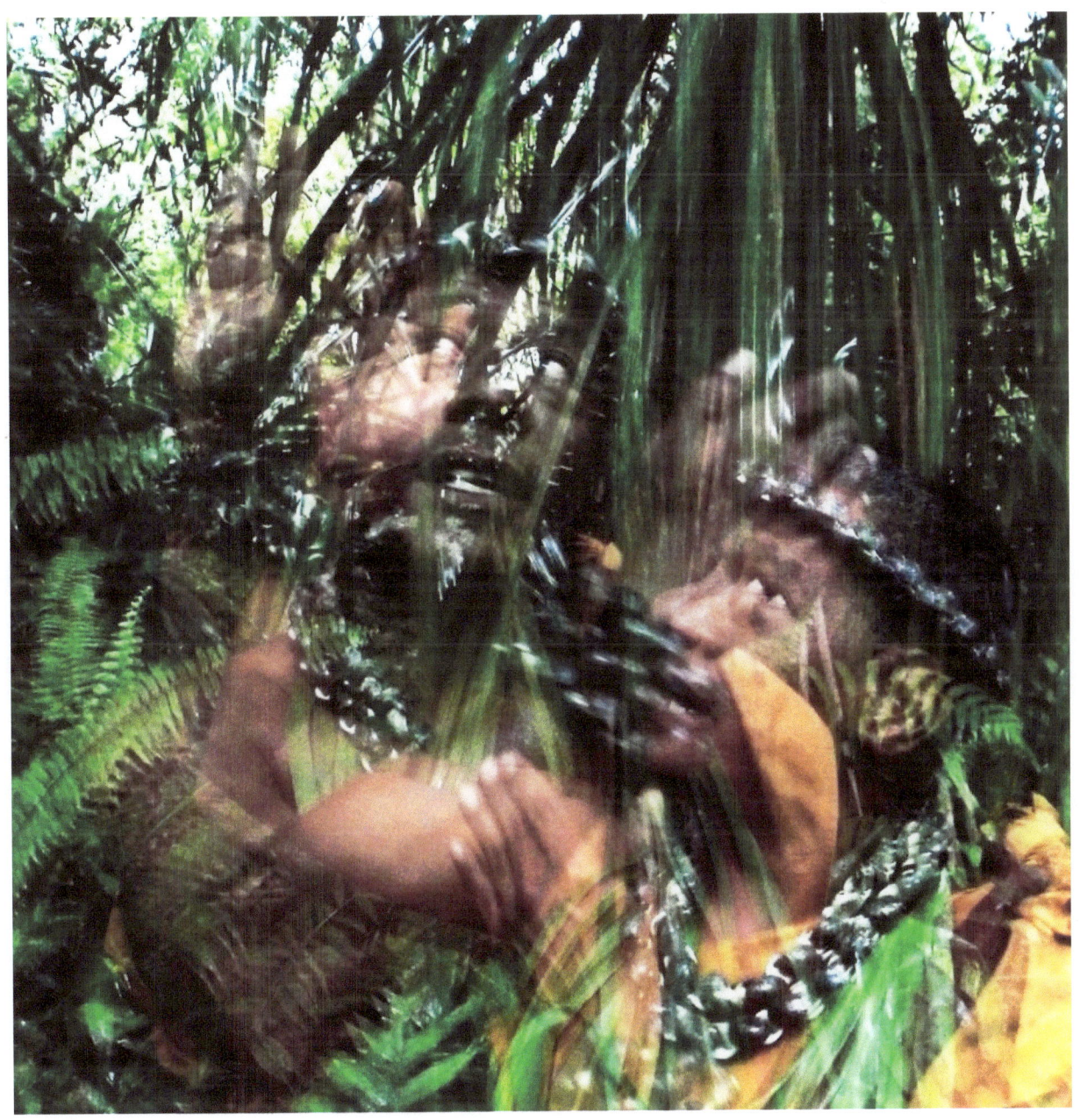

Lava Caves and Tubes

Chapter Three

Preservation of this area is in honor of, and reverence for, Volcano Fire Goddess Pelehonuamea . . . often simply referred to as Pele or Tūtū Pele.

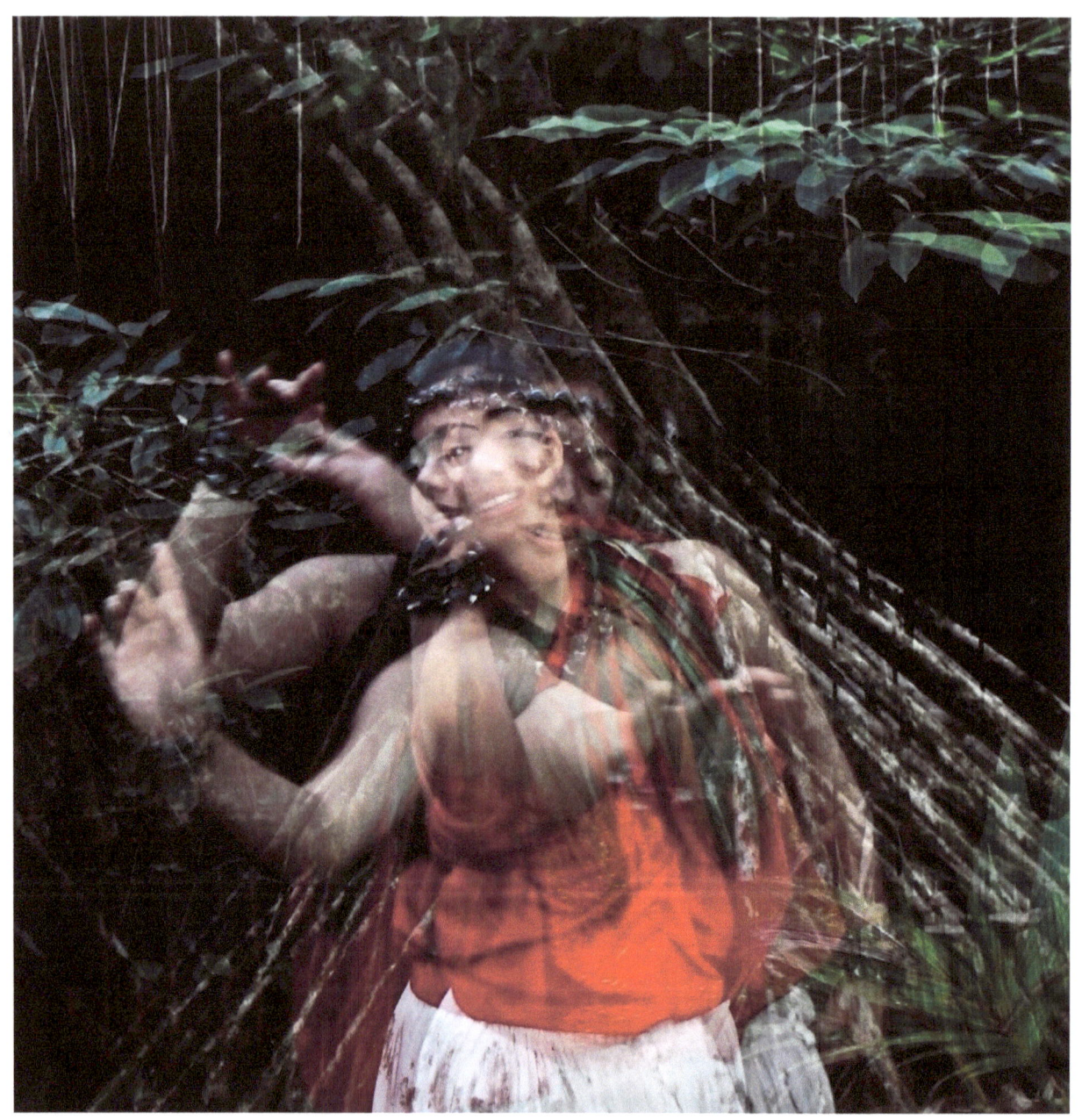

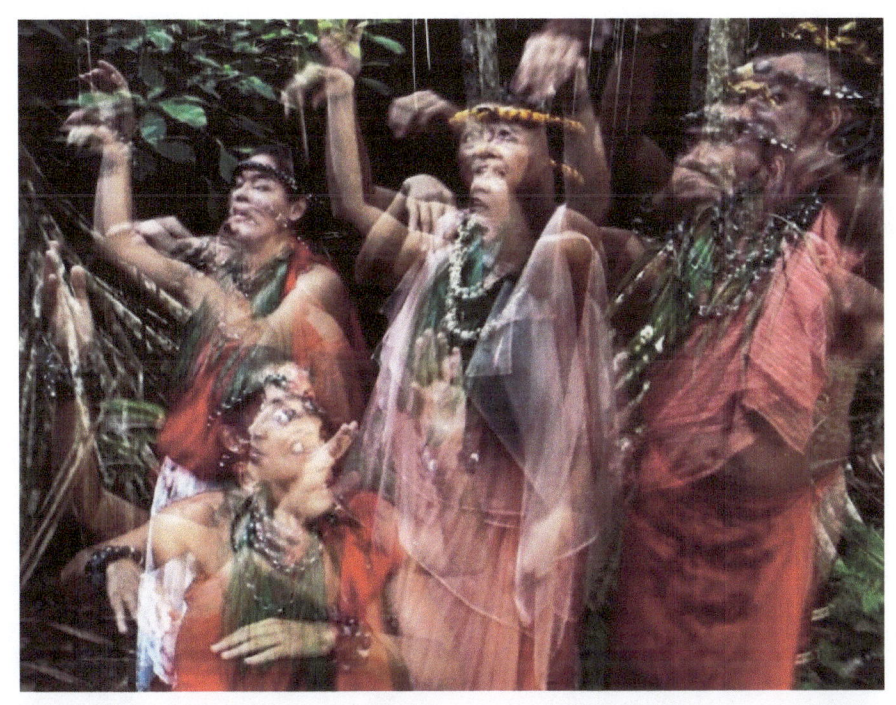

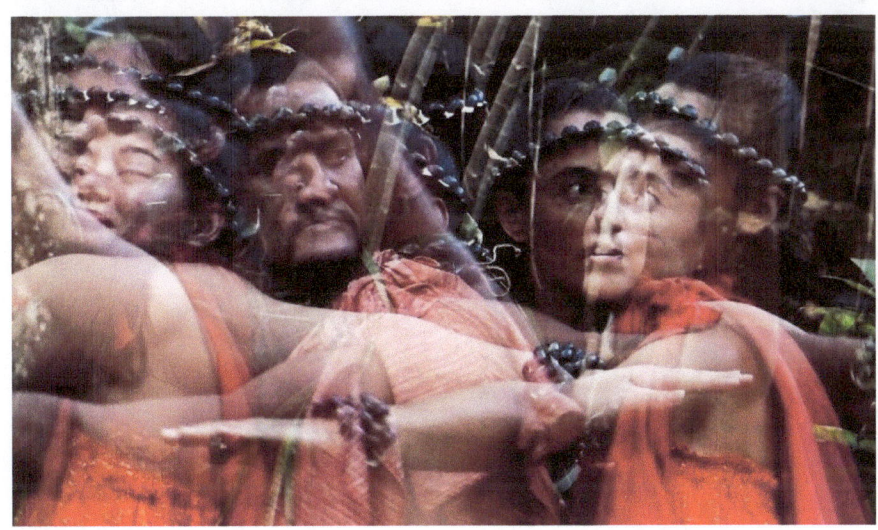

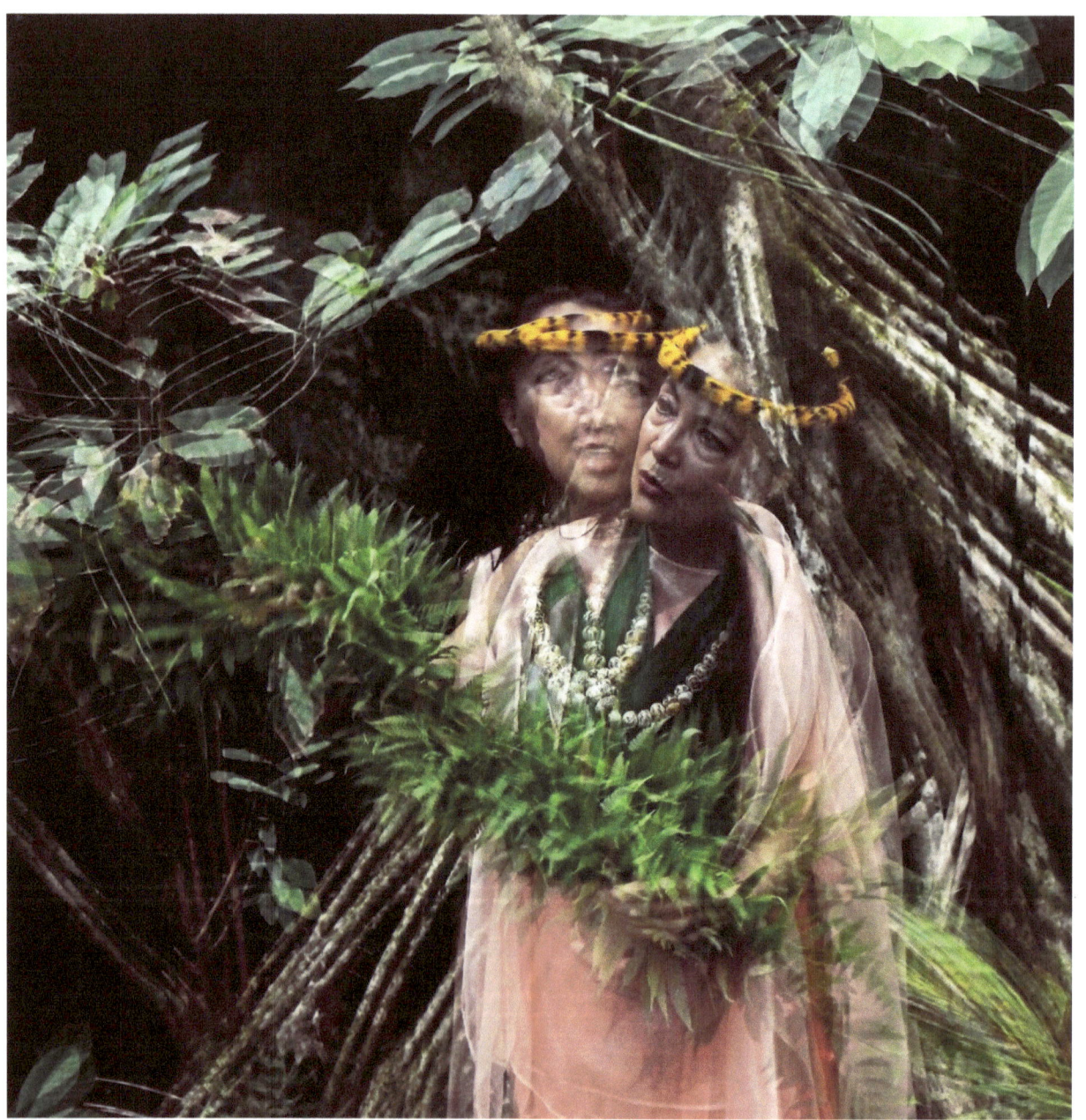

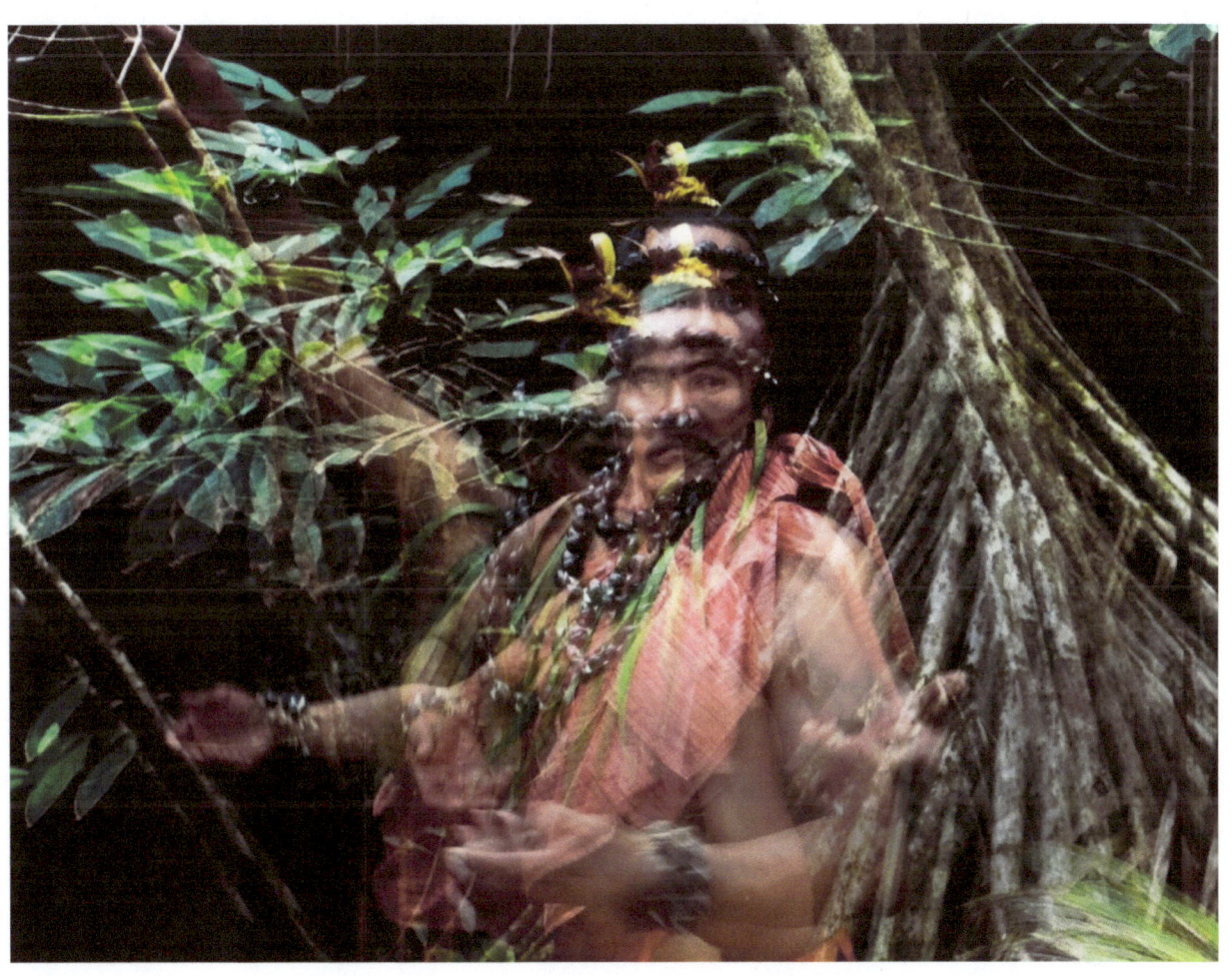

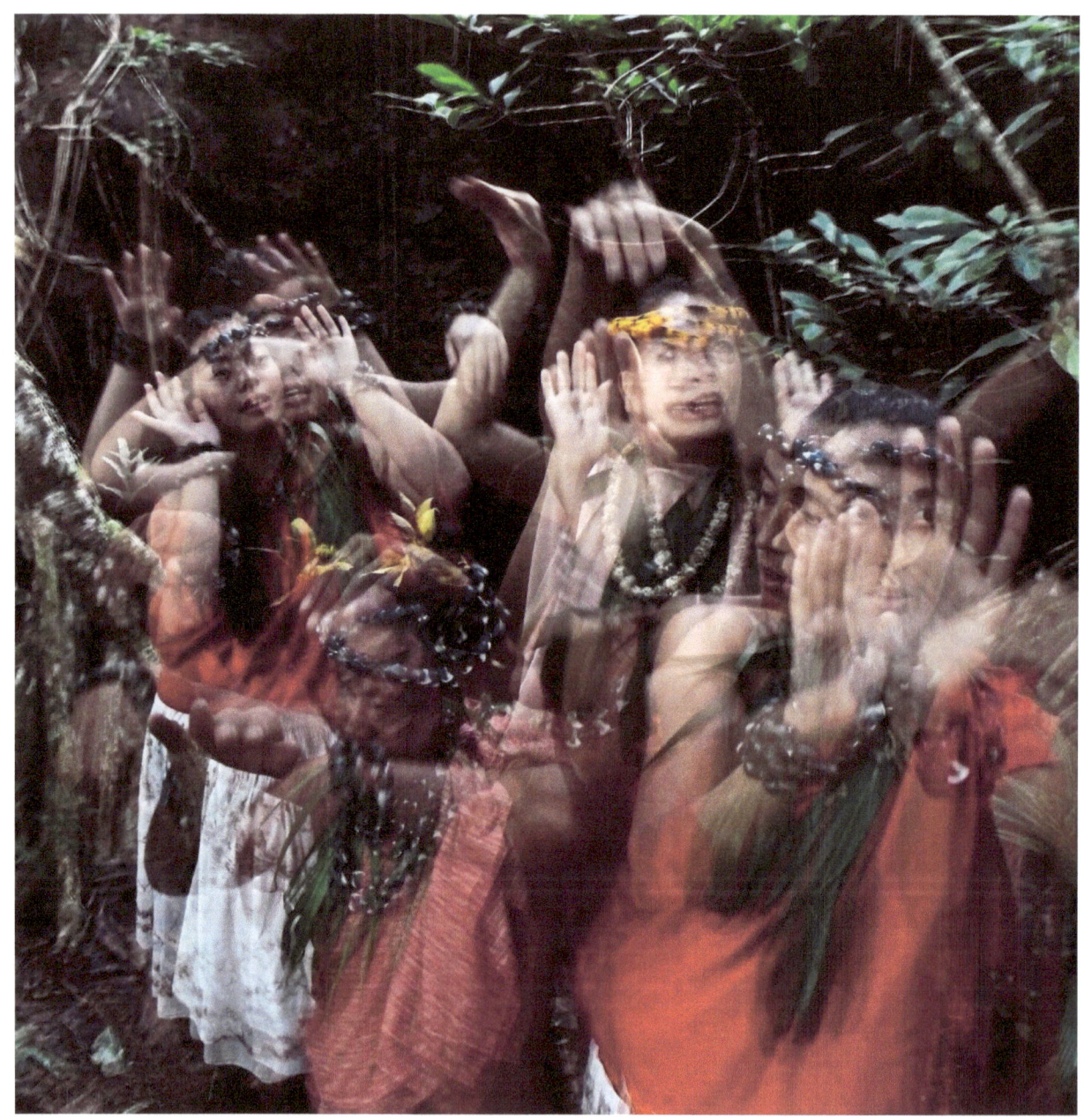

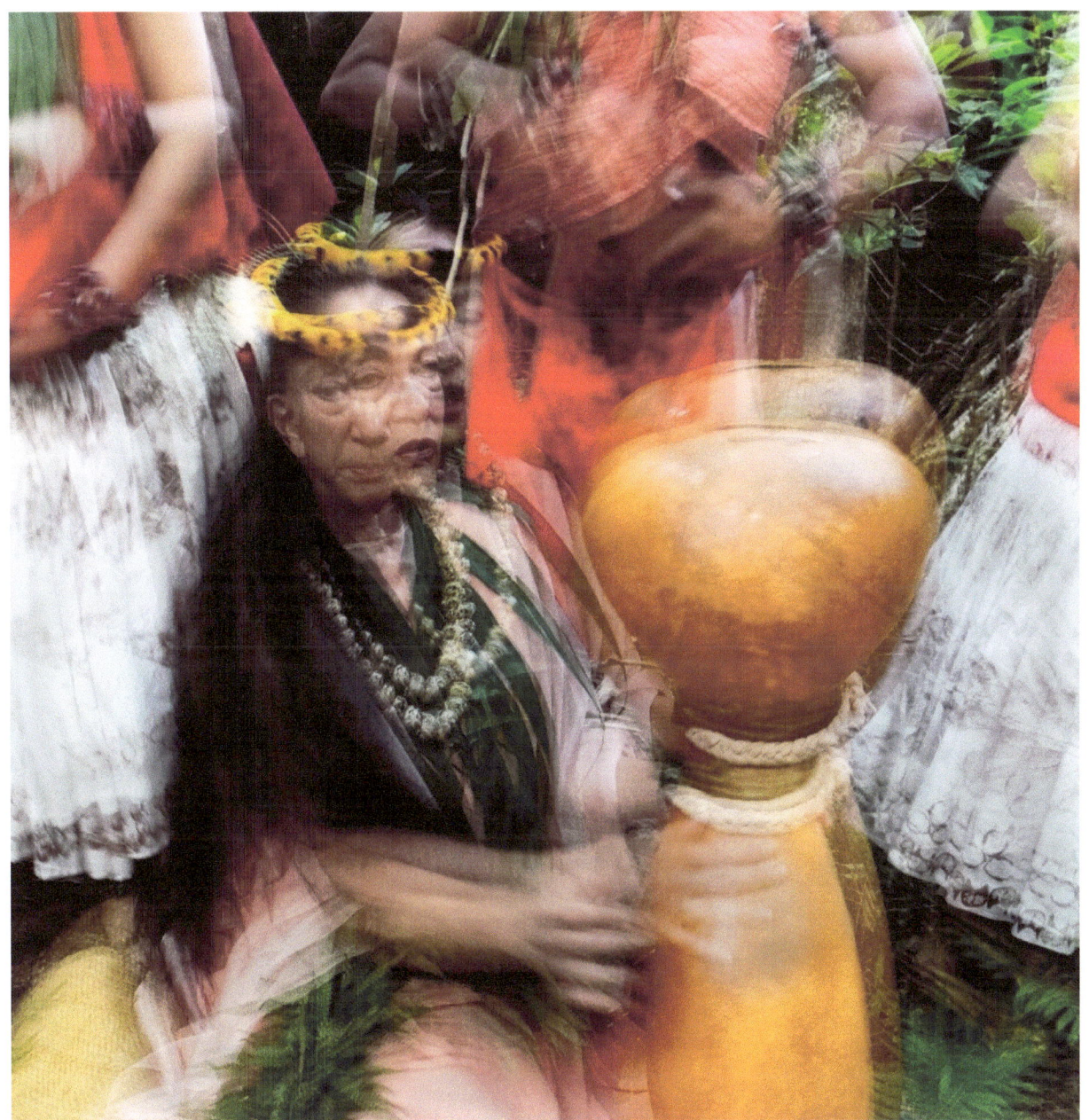

A Sacred Temple
Chapter Four

The place name is Kukii Heiau, an astrological temple built around 1500 AD. The Hawaiian people are said to be among the first astronomers, calling upon the stars, planets, sun, moon, and other parts of nature to guide them on traveling across the sea. Tradition also says the *heiau* was used for *'apu k ōheoheo* (poisoning) by the *kahuna* (priest). In 1877, King David Kalakaua brought some of the flat, large stones to Honolulu to be used in constructing the foundation of the 'Iolani Palace.

One of Kumu's missions is to restore not only this *heiau*, but others as well, out of respect for the ancestors.

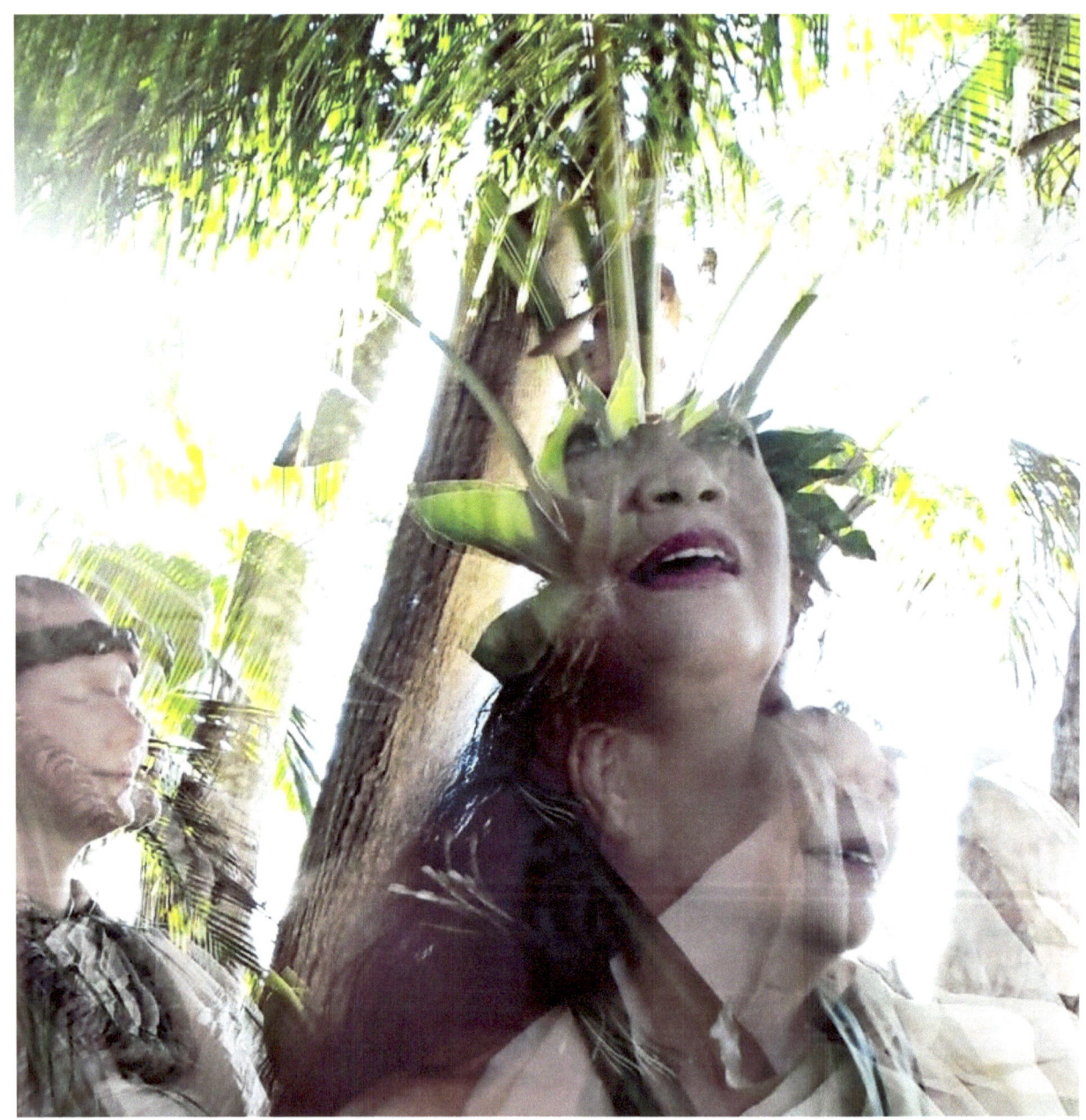

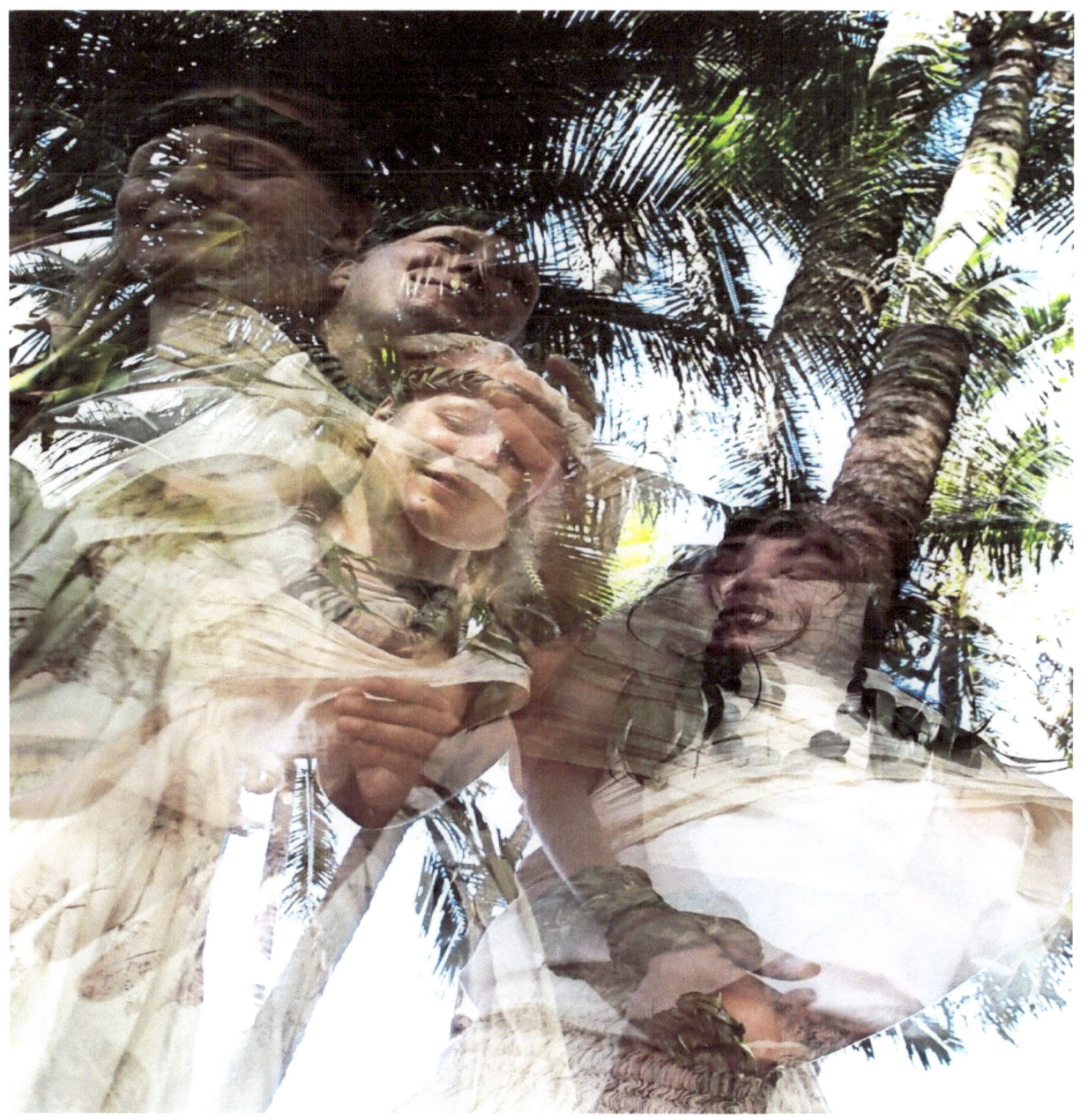

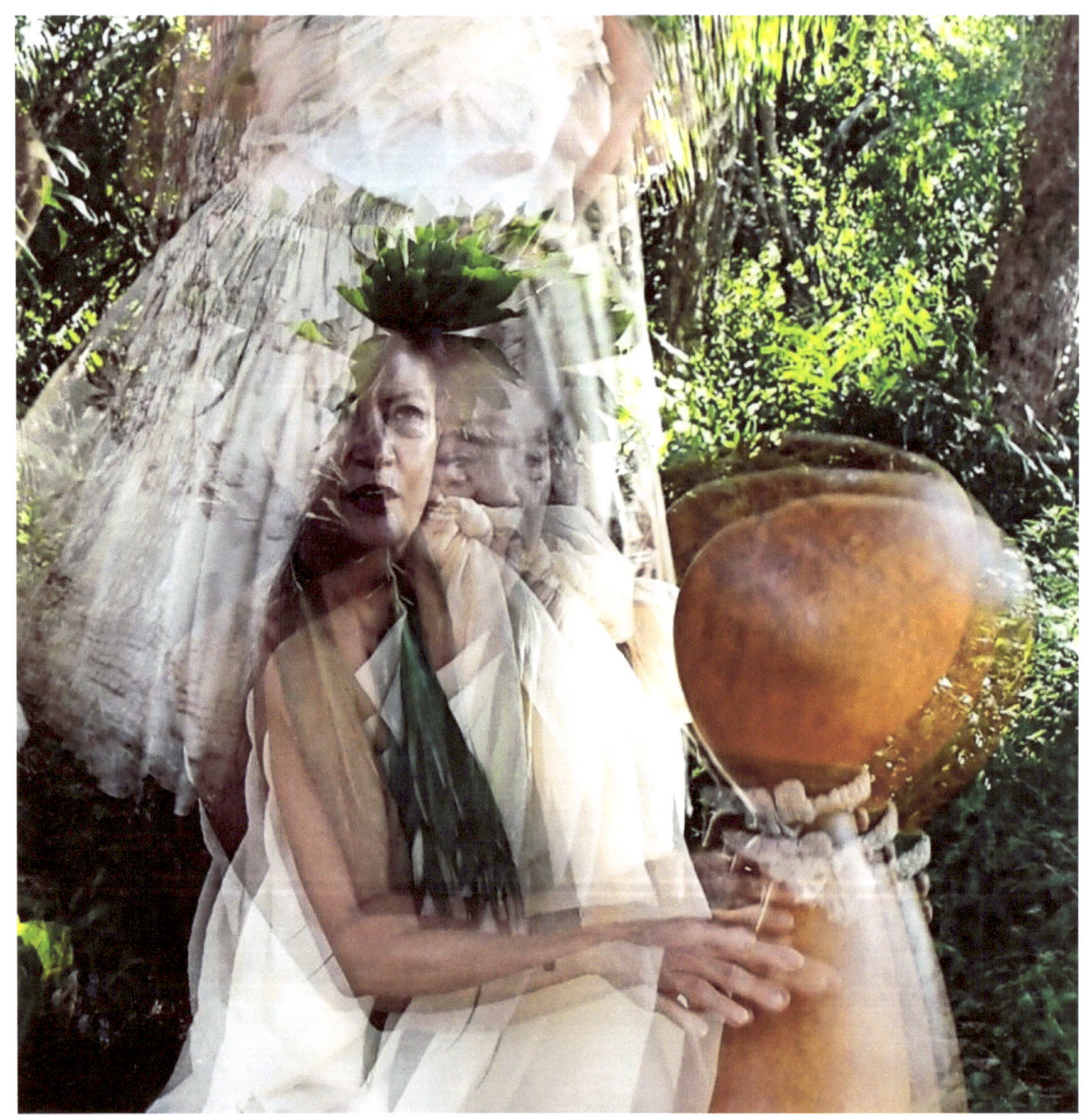

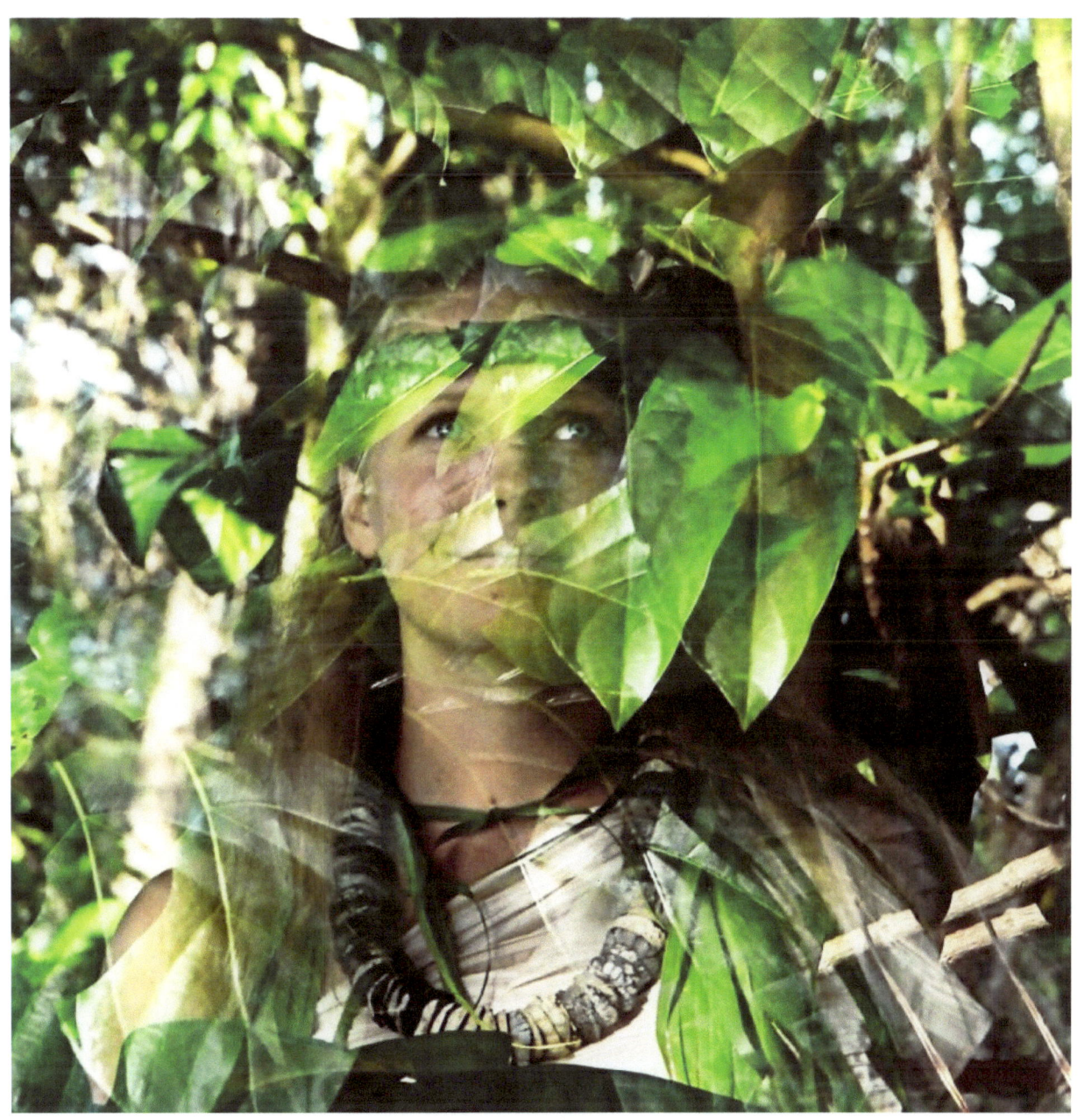

Volcanoes

Chapter Five

Halemaʻumaʻu crater is in the caldera, a small crater within the large crater of Kilauea Volcano, home of the Volcano Fire Goddess Pelehonuamea.

The volcano historically and at present inspires a great deal of respect, due to its activity and power. From the vantage point of the summit of Kilauea in Hawaiʻi's Volcanoes National Park one can view the Halemaʻumaʻu Crater. Halemaʻumaʻu has been erupting consistently since the crater became active again in March 2008. Its lava creates the newest land on earth, when it plunges into the sea to expand Big Island Hawaiʻi. In its presence, it is easy to recognize why it was named the home of a great fire goddess.

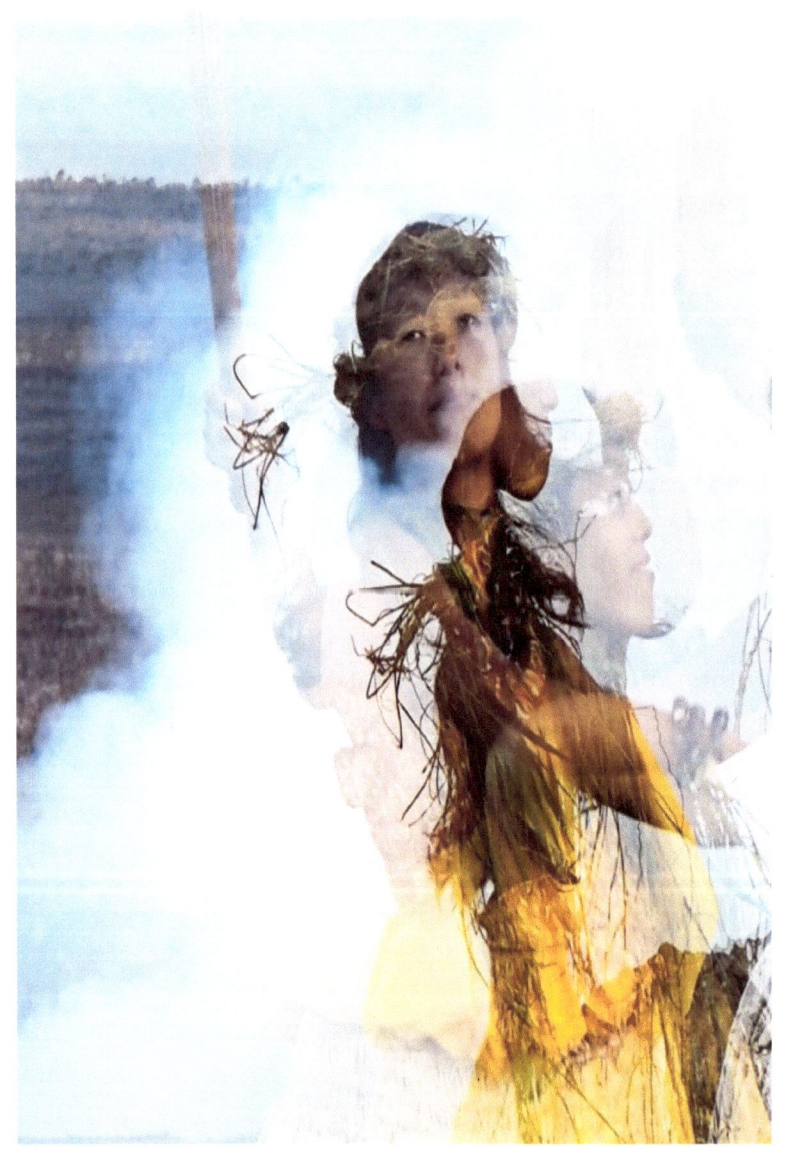

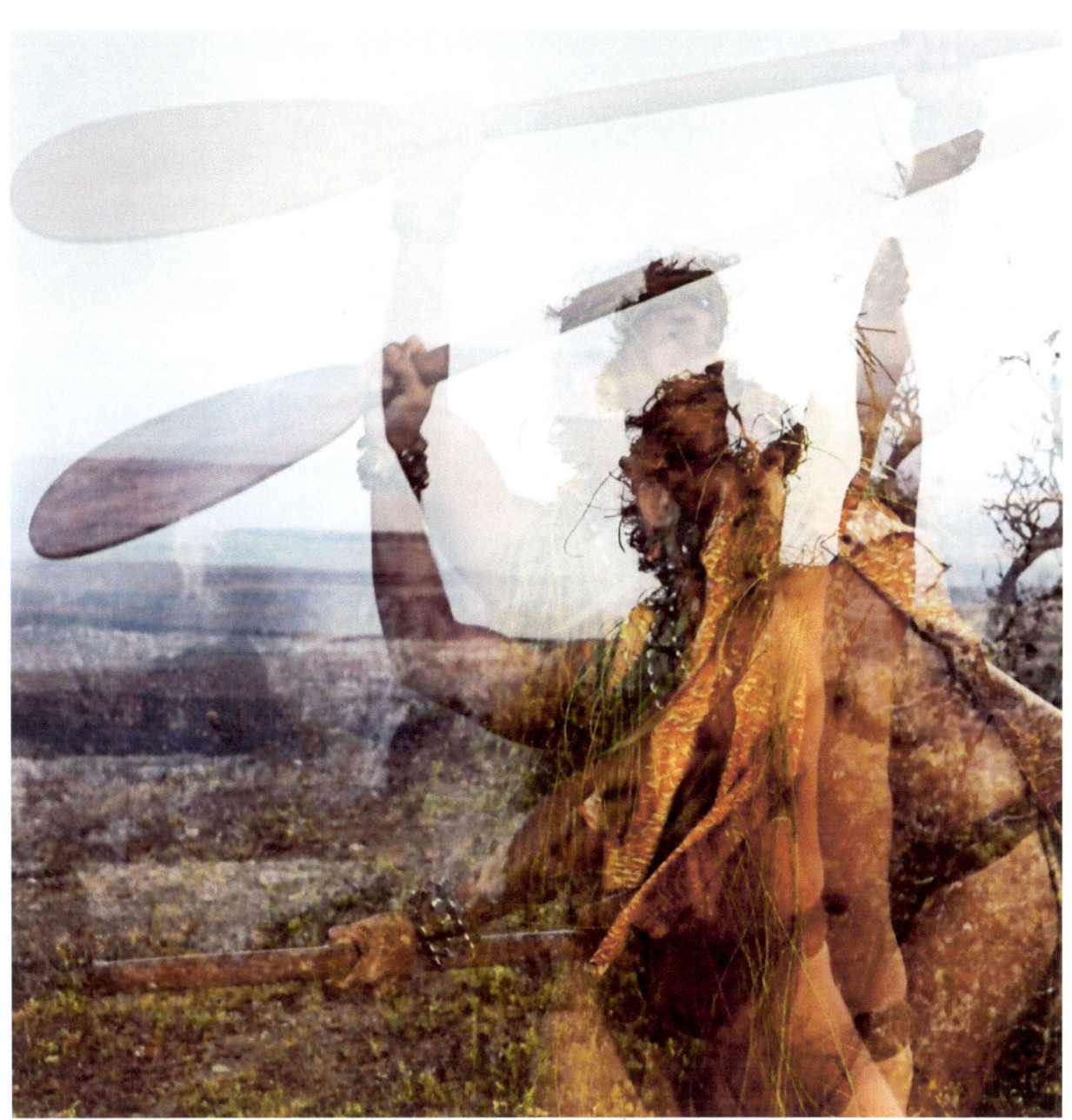

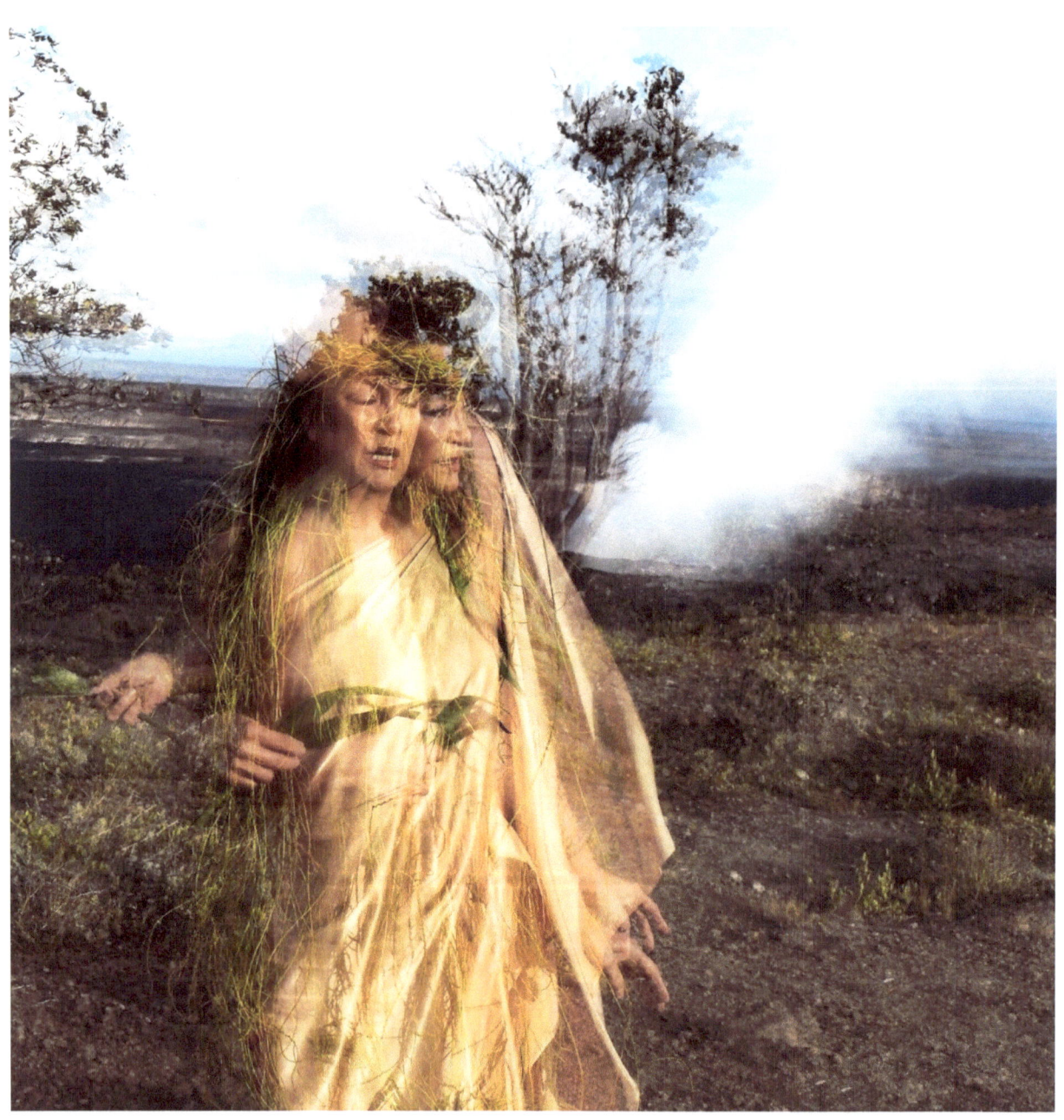

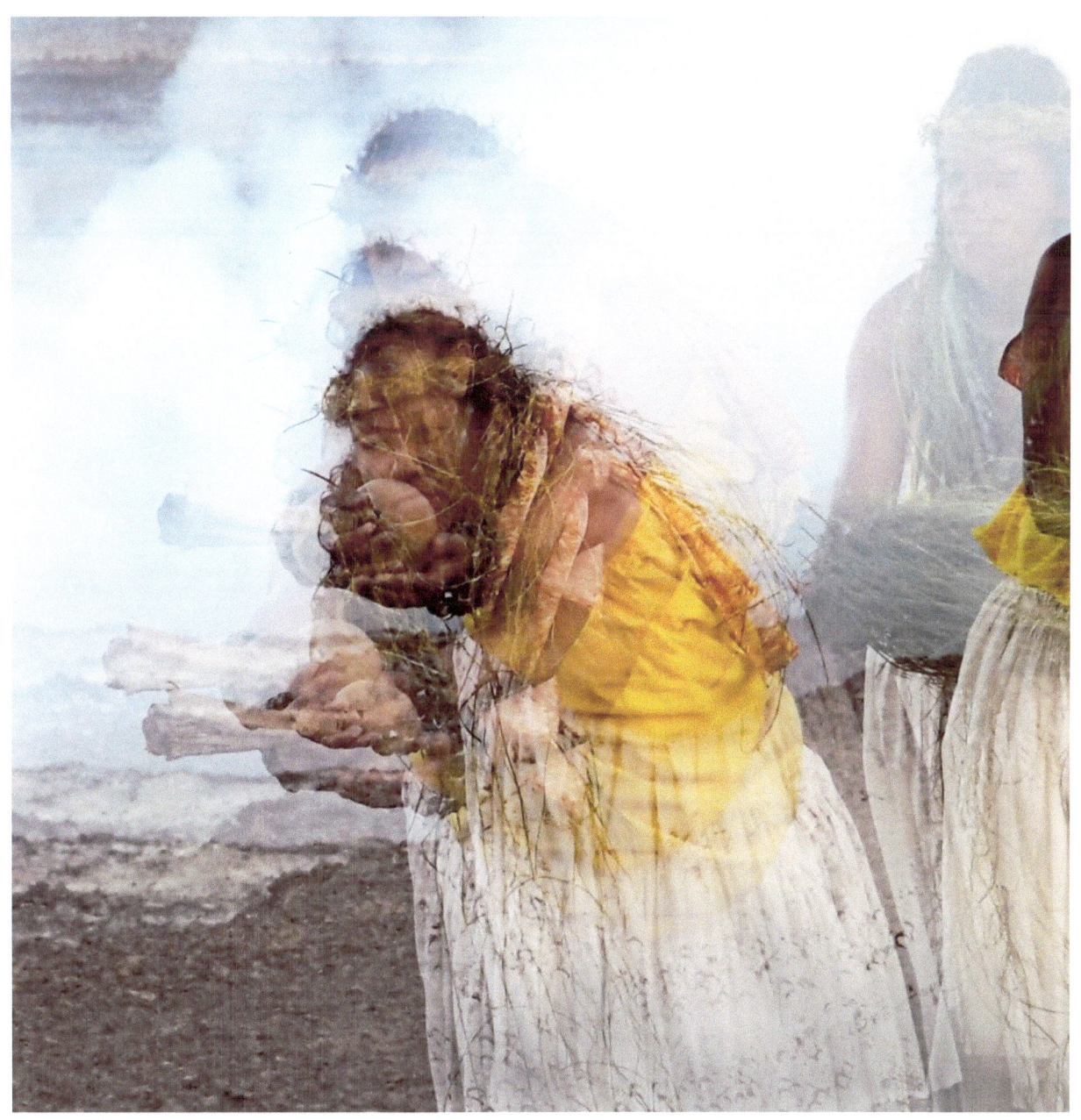

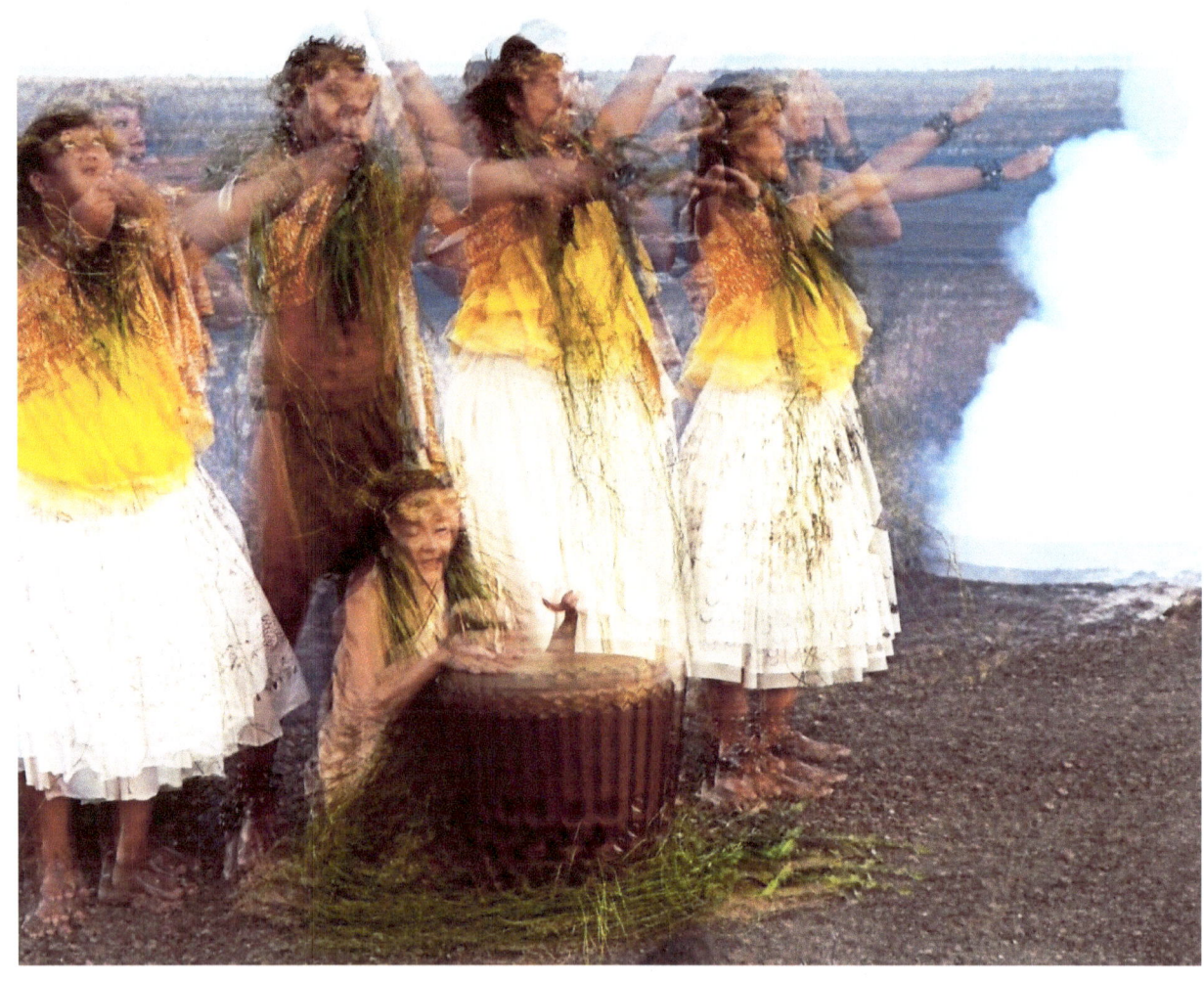

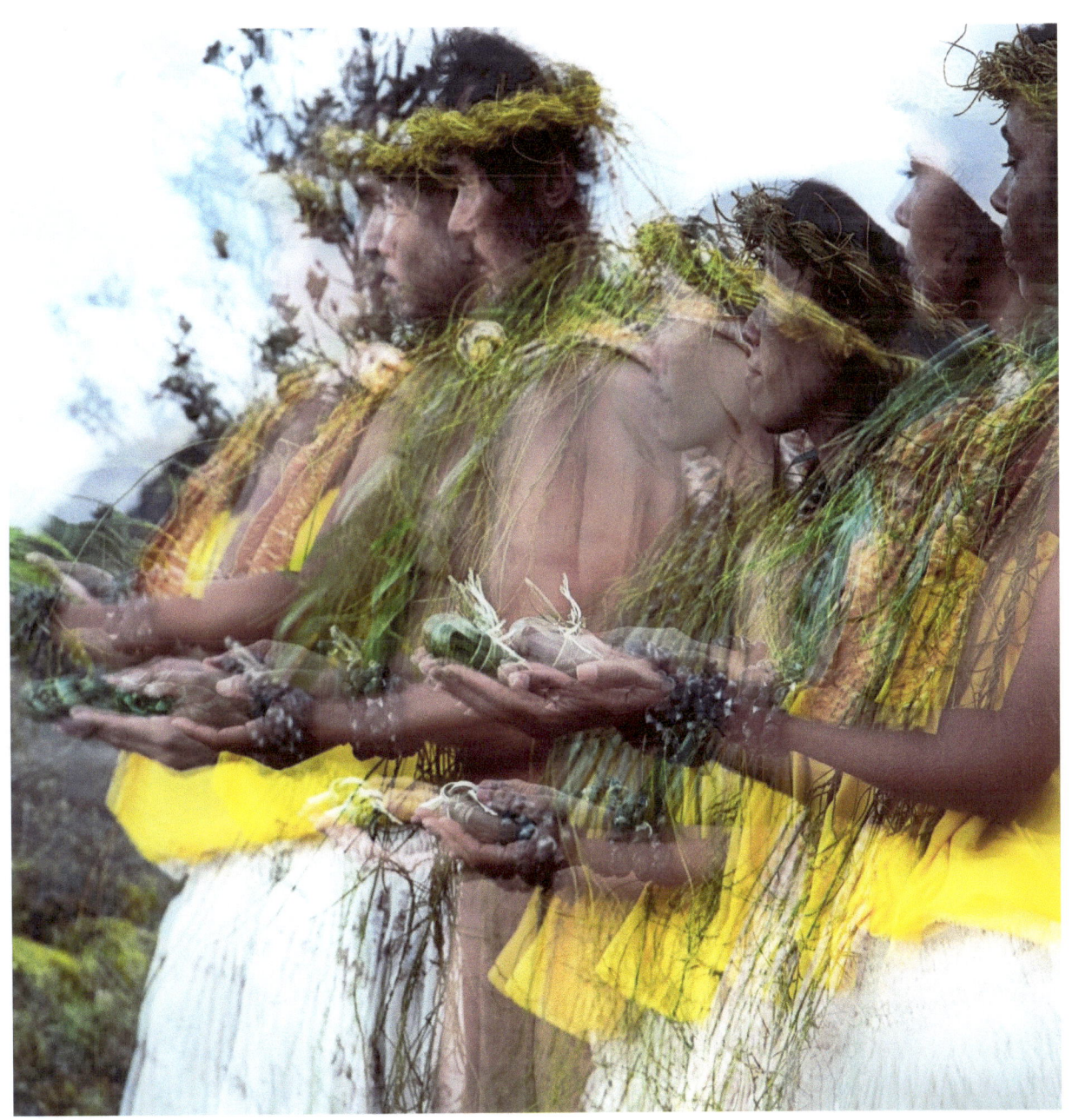

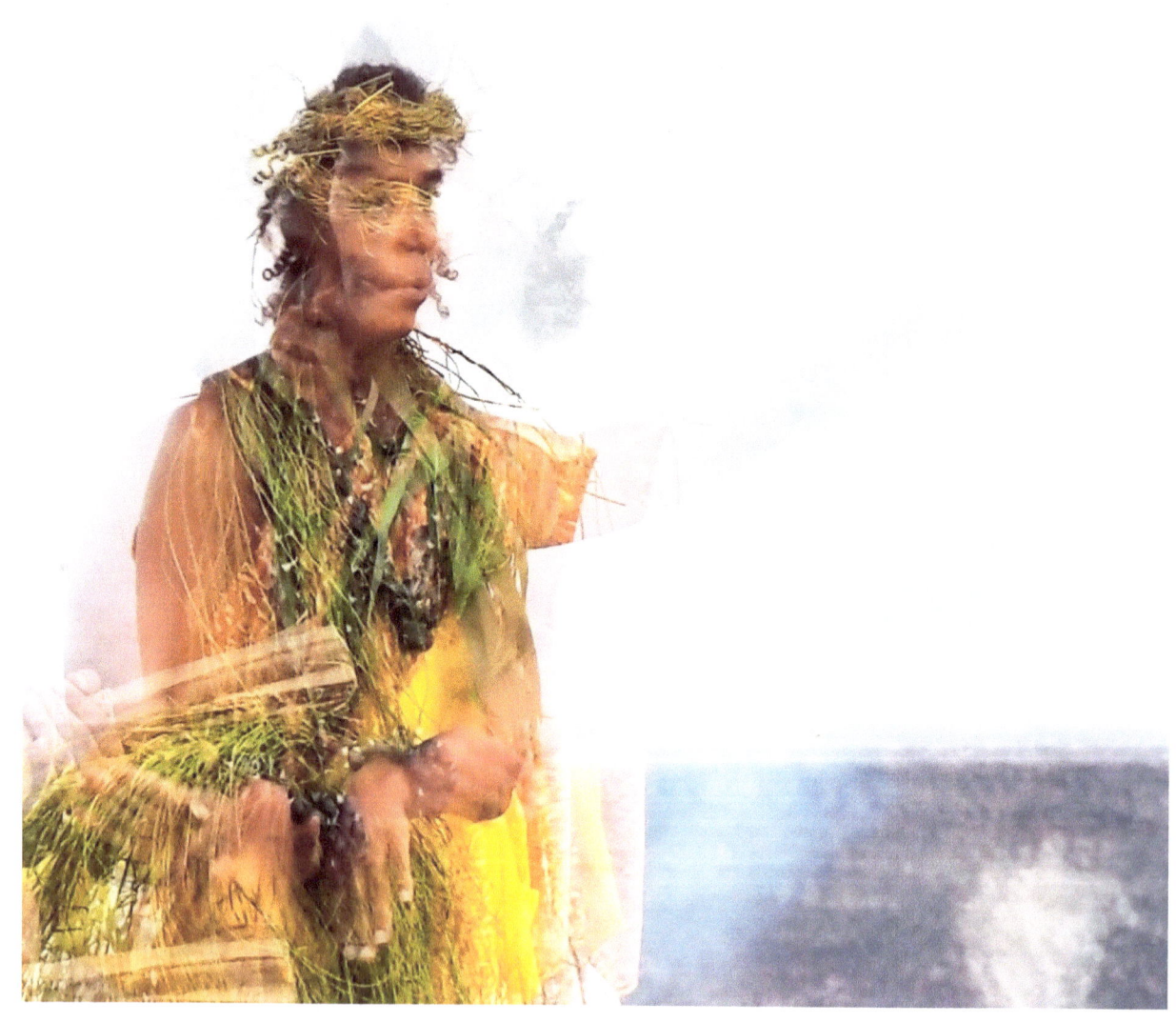

Participating dancers (na haumanu)

Kauʻilani Quihano

Kuaneʻomea Cariaga

Akeakamai Zamora

Moani Metter

Ulumahiehie Gomes

Uʻilani Pihana

Kawaiʻapo Dusschee

Lilinoe Stark

Kimo Lopez

Andrena White

Makalei Arakaki

Kumu Hula Aliʻi Kahuna Nui Ehulani Stephany

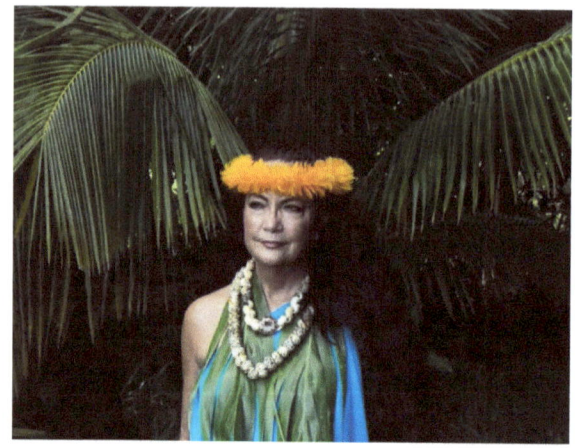

Kumu Biography

I started *hula* as an adult, not earlier. When I was growing up our Hawaiian culture was dying or undercover, therefore I did not learn about it in school—no history, no language, no chants, no *hula*, no protocol, unless it was for May Day. This was a special day in the year, May 1st, where the Hawaiian culture was honored. All the schools in the islands would celebrate. We would wear flower *leis* and Hawaiian clothing. We would share the *hula* and host a Hawaiian Royal Court.

Children were selected to represent our *Mōʻī kane*, and *Mōʻī Wahine* (kings and queens) along with their royal attendants. All the classes would share together in a large gathering for parents and guests to come enjoy. When I moved to the island of Hawaiʻi in 1976, I was becoming very drawn to learn about the *hula* and about our Hawaiian culture. I studied *hula*, chant, culture, and protocol with 14 different *Kumu Hula*, which was a great blessing for me. To get deeper into our Hawaiian culture, I took on studies at Hawaiʻi Community College. And I gained a deeper knowledge, studying with the Kanakaʻole ʻohana and other knowledgeable Hawaiian practitioners. I also received a degree in Hawaiian culture and hula.

I felt a deep yearning to know more about the *hula kahiko* (ancient hula). I participated in many different types of *hula* competitions and found it was not for me. I felt that a competition changes the true meaning of *hula*. I came to realize that *hula kahiko* brings out the sacredness. I'm guided at all times with our ancestors, helping and blessing me with all that I do.

Long ago the only way that Hawaiian people would write any history was with petroglyphs. The full history came through in chants and *hula*. The chant conveys oral history, the dance expands its meaning, sharing the true meaning and feeling of *Aloha* and spreading this feeling throughout the world. (Kumu travels to Japan, New Zealand and Australia as well, establishing relations with other indigenous stewards of our earth.)

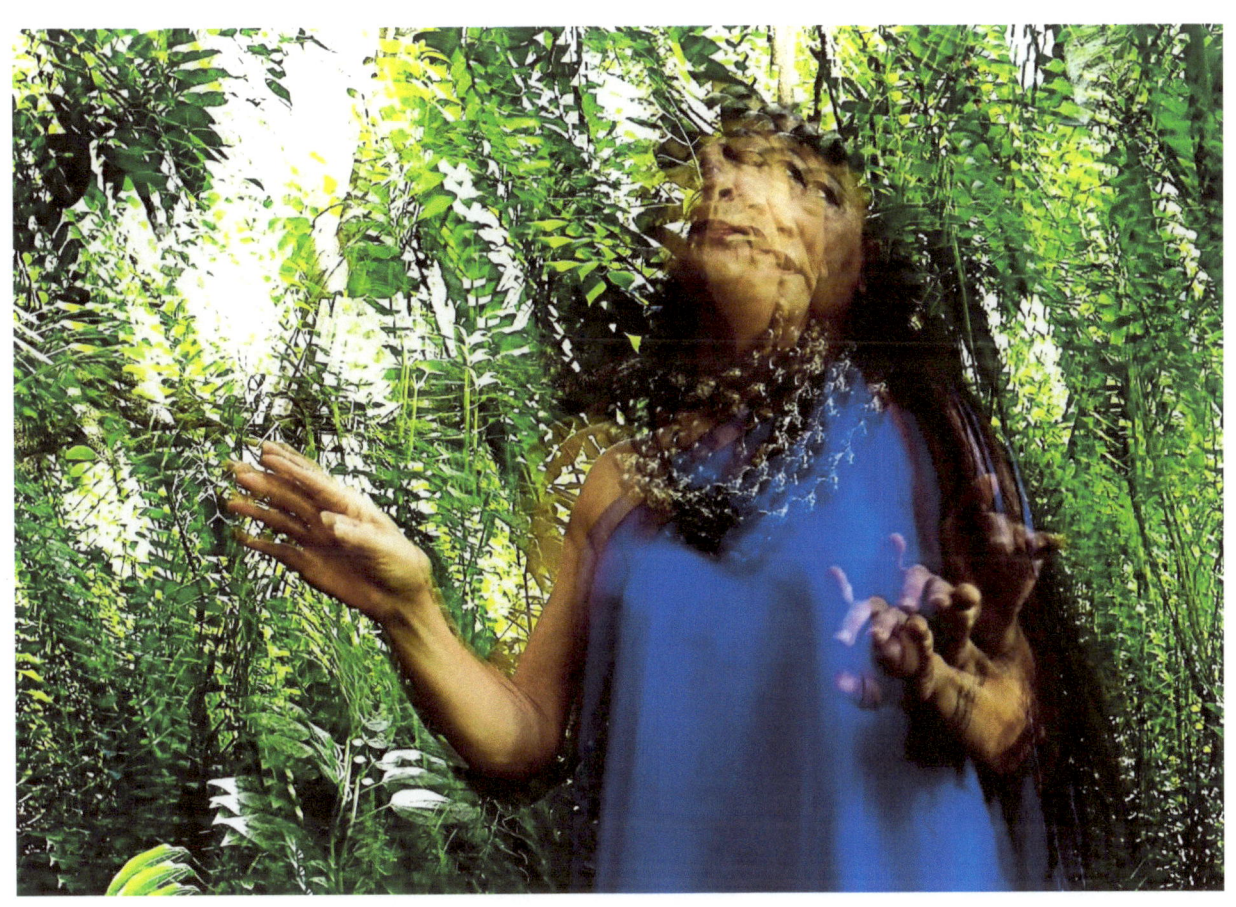

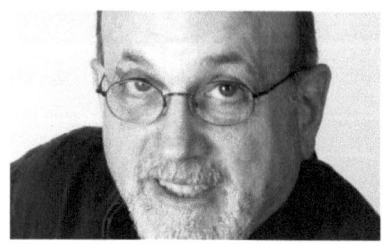

Author Biography

Michael Philip Manheim has been a professional photographer since 1969. His early work is journalistic in nature, and those skills he developed in reflexively recording human nature evolved into the fine art photography he creates today. Manheim's photographs are held in private and public collections including the Library of Congress, the International Photography Hall of Fame, the National Archives, the Danforth Museum of Art, and the Bates College Museum of Art

"[Manheim's photographs] have passion and beauty, and clearly considerable skill has gone into their execution."
— *Julian Cox, Founding Curator of Photography and Chief Administrative Curator of the Fine Arts Museums of San Francisco*

For full bio go to: michaelphilipmanheim.com/MPM-biography.php

behance.net/michaelphilipmanheim

www.ingramcontent.com/pod-product-compliance
Lightning Source LLC
Chambersburg PA
CBHW050901180526
45159CB00007B/2753